Trudging Through Yesterday's Britain

Trudging Through Yesterday's Britain by Chris Staverson.

Copyright © Chris Staverson. December 2022.

This paperback edition first published December 2022.

Second edition published January 2023.

Third edition published April 2023.

This fourth edition published July 2023.

This title is also available for Kindle.

By the same author:

Whatever Will Be, Will Be – the true story of my French adventure in the year 2000.

Getting Off The Estate – Part 1 of the 'Changing Lives' series. A fictional account following the lives of two boys, who live on the same council estate in south-east England.

It Started In Margate – A black comedy.

Introduction.

When I was born the swinging sixties were almost done for. That decade of feeling good, highlighted by the radical change in musical style and attitudes, was about to be consigned to history, to be replaced by the seventies and all that came with those ten years of hardship and uncertainty. If the sixties had given people a reason to be alive, the seventies would wipe the smile off of their faces. If the sixties had been about letting go, the seventies would be about being reeled back in. The sixties gave people hope after the fifties. The seventies would give us nothing to write home about.

But growing up in the seventies meant nothing to me. How could I compare it to a decade that I knew nothing of? My parents spoke fondly of the previous decade, saying that it was probably the best time of their lives. Dad was in the Royal Marines, and had enjoyed an overseas posting in Singapore. Mum had been out there with him, and every now and then they would delight in getting out the old photograph albums and reminiscing about those golden days. I have a framed photo of my father wearing his military uniform, with his rifle slung over his shoulder, and him smiling. My mother is standing next to him. Their eyes are full of joy. It must have been the greatest of times for them. But nothing good lasts forever.

My earliest memories are of going to primary school and singing in the assembly. I used to wear short trousers to school, even in deepest winter. It was a terrible place, which has since been demolished. Expensive flats now stand on the field where I used to run in the egg and spoon race on sports day. And then there was that bloody indoor swimming pool, filled with tepid water, which went up to our waists. It was there where I tried to learn to swim, to no avail. The building in which the pool was located had a leaking roof, so every now and then the school would have fund-raising events to bring people through its doors, hoping that they would give enough money to fix the roof.

Dad, by now, was working in a factory and mother worked a few hours a week in the local branch of Marks and Spencer. Together, with my older brother, we lived in a council house. The estate on which we lived was a typical estate from that era, where the houses boasted front and back gardens. Our house was at the end of a terrace, so we had a bigger back garden than the other tenants living in the row. But it was a massive change to what they had been used to. Dad always seemed tired when he came home from work, and mother was often irritable. And I remember when dad was working only three days a week, and power cuts were a frequent occurrence. We would eat by candlelight, and it all seemed so much fun – but it wasn't.

Back then Christmases seemed to go on forever. They were great times for me, but not so for my parents. They would have struggled to put food on the table and pay the rent. But at Christmastime all of those worries seemed to evaporate for a few weeks. The sacrifices they must have made were enormous. And after Christmas it was back to school, with a new coat and brand new shoes. There were so many things that I took for granted back then, because as a child I could only see as far as the end of my nose. I had no idea just how bad things were. But it wasn't all doom and gloom, was it?

I'm just an ordinary man with a simple tale to tell. I'm sure many of you who will read this book, or who follow me on Twitter, can relate to my memories. Indeed, on Twitter it seems that my childhood memories are shared by thousands of others in my age group. I seem to have opened up a lot of old photograph albums in peoples' minds. Of course, some people believe that whilst nostalgia is a great thing, it's only the future that counts. This might be true, but the past can't be brushed under the carpet, and it shouldn't be discarded.

So join me on a journey to my past, in which I have tried to recall some good and bad times from my childhood and subsequent years. In this book the story ends when I'm in my early thirties, when a massive change occurred in my life. What happened after is material for a second book. I'll let you decide if yesterday's Britain was a better Britain, or if it was worse than the Britain of today. One thing is sure, and that is yesterday's Britain was certainly different, and if life was harder back then, it couldn't have been any worse than the period today's Britain is going through. Back then there were turbulent times and times of discontent, but today the road ahead looks far from smooth. Britain, sadly, is in a terrible mess, struggling to find its place in the world. A once united kingdom is now dislocated, and resembles a nation on the verge of revolution. Ordinary, hard-working people are now accustomed to visiting food banks to put food on their tables, and those same people no longer have the financial power to heat their homes. Cut off from Europe by Brexit, Great Britain is now laughed at and ridiculed by countries which once looked up to it. The desire to be independent was so overbearing that the consequences of leaving Europe weren't even considered. And now, several years after the divorce, many British people are wishing that Britain was still part of the club.

1: Deceit. 1993.

I remember THAT day as if it was yesterday, which is an achievement in itself considering the amount of booze I've downed in the intermediate years. I remember the bastards who tried to shit on me from a great height, and I recall the darkest days when I believed that those same bastards would get the better of me. And then I remember how it all began, in 1993, and how circumstances, twists and turns, fate, the alignment of the planets and simple destiny took me from there to here. But when I say 1993, I mean that's when everything slotted into place and when the tick-tock of the countdown clock started its seven-year ticking and tocking until the year 2000, and my liberation from the dogs and vermin who had made my life hell.

Oh, yes, I had done well for a boy with just two 'O' levels, for what I lacked in academic qualifications I made up for with the gift of the gab. I could, and still can, lie as if I really believed that it was the truth spilling from my mouth. You see, if you convince yourself that lies are really the truth, when you come to tell them your facial expressions won't betray you. I can spot liars from a mile away, in the manner that they might straighten their ties, scratch the side of their faces and refuse to look at you as they hopelessly fumble their way through a pack of untruths. Of course, lying to get through life is frowned upon, but if the world is full of decent people languishing in the depths of mediocrity, it's because they've convinced themselves that honesty is the best policy.

I should never had got the job back then, because my curriculum vitae was two pages of untruths and my past was less than inspiring. On that day, when the chief bastard interviewed me, I was running on adrenalin and cigarettes. And the chief bastard liked to think that he was the smartest man in the room, which logically meant that he should have seen straight through me. But dear Alan must have been having a bad day, because he seemed to swallow all of the shit I was spewing out, sitting in his corner office, in the charming cathedral town of Canterbury. If only he had checked with my last employer, who didn't exist, he would have saved himself from a lot of grief seven years down the line. God was smiling down on me that day, and on the next occasion when I returned for a second interview and more questioning. Alan was impressed and offered me the job. The pay was minimal but the opportunities to advance were unlimited. I just had to keep my nose clean, my head down and get on with the job. It all sounded so easy, but it was not to be. I hoped that I had at last found something good to build upon, but I hadn't. The next seven years were to be sheer hell, but how could I complain when I had lied my way into the job?

My ill-fitting suit, bought in a sale from a High Street menswear shop, said all that there was to say about me. It spoke of a poor young man who had finally, through cunning and guile, got himself a job to be proud of. The road to there hadn't been easy, but then again, as my train shuddered to a halt, I told myself that an easy life is probably a dull life. The rain intensified as I jogged out of the station, hoping to get to the office before a torrential downpour ruined my ninety-nine pound bargain. I ran along the bridge and through the park, where on that day other people were also on their way to work. My jacket was open and it flapped in the damp air, as the Almighty one decided to have some first-day-in-the-new-job fun with me. The skies opened wider and I was drenched before I finally got to the office. Out of the summer rain I composed myself, and I thought about the next suit I was going to buy. It was going to be a hundred times better that the cheap tat in which I was dressed.

I wasn't looking to set the world on fire, but I wanted something that would put a huge wedge between my uneventful and depressing past, and what I hoped was going to be a glimmering future. I wanted to be one of those well-dressed people who others looked at in the park, as they ran along in their cheap suits and new plastic shoes. I wanted to be the one who turned heads and made people stop and think. I wanted to shake off the past, which was loaded with false promises and failure, in which I had edged along like an old car, not quite ready for the scrapheap but not good enough to to blaze a trail. I wanted to wipe clean the slate, and do something with my life.

And I thought that I had finally arrived on the rainy May day, in 1993. Alan had given me the chance to put the record straight. Alan had liked what I had said, nodding his head occasionally as I spewed out more and more bullshit. I liked Alan, and thought that he was my saviour. HE was the one who had given this young man from a council estate some hope. But it was all to be another massive deception. It was going to be a seven-year saga that I didn't spot coming, although the warning signs had been clear to see. The misery was set to linger, but, and as they say in France, *c'est la vie!*

2: Summer – 1976.

I have sketchy memories of my early years, that sometimes come to me in the night in monochrome dreams. I do recall all of the Christmases that I lived through as a small child, and I remember the weeks I spent out of school, stretched out in my bed, trying to get over asthma. That was a real spanner in my childhood works, which left me wheezing and spluttering, tucked up under tight-fitting blankets, reading and sleeping, or sleeping and reading. Science has come on in leaps and bounds since the early seventies, but back then the cure for asthma was putting a plastic capsule in an inhaler, and breathing in as hard as my feeble state would allow, taking in the white powder that the capsule contained. The inhaler made a whirring sound as it propelled the powder down my throat, and it was a regular feature in my early years. My doctor would make the occasional visit to the house, if I was really bad, and it took me years to finally shake off the debilitating malady. In my early twenties I took to smoking cigarettes and small cigars, and whenever my mother saw me lighting up a cigarette, she would sometimes ask me if I remembered being very poorly with asthma, and if I thought smoking was a good idea. Well, of course, it wasn't a very intelligent thing to do, but as smoking went together with my other new hobby, drinking, giving up that bloody filthy habit was going to take some doing.

When I was incapacitated during the summer months, my bedroom window would be left slightly open, so slithers of warm air could caress my face. In the garden, mother would drink tea with her sister, sometimes returning to the house, to shout from the bottom of the stairs enquiring if I was okay. I would drink orange squash by the bucketful, but my poor appetite left me content to eat a sandwich every now and then, but nothing more. Those bedridden days would turn into weeks, and whilst dad would go to work at the factory, and mother would do her hours at the local branch of Marks and Spencer, I would be alone, looking up at my bedroom ceiling, or sleeping through those long summer hours. Dad would come in and see if I was okay, and mother would bring me orange squash and comics. I had a transistor radio that I used to enjoy tuning in to obscure stations, listening to plays or Jimmy Young on Radio Two.

I remember the summer of 1976, like those asthma-filled days, as if it was only yesterday. It stands out like a beacon, begging to be revisited, relived and re-loved, in a way that a defining year in anyone's childhood should be. Anyone lucky to be alive during THAT year will have so many memories to tell, even if, in reality, the scorching summer was a short-lived affair, eventually being wiped out by traditional heavy rainfalls and thunder storms. Back then a Mediterranean-style heatwave was a rare occurrence, but today, decades later, we are are more accustomed to blazing hot summers and mild winters, produced by global warming, which was already taking shape five decades ago. Of course, global warming is a result of us human beings relying more and more on power-consuming gadgets and fuel-guzzling forms of transport. Our coal-fired power stations of the past were already pumping out tonnes of toxic clouds into the sky, so it's not a new phenomenon. Our old factories were discharging the same shit and grime into the air, but no-one realised back then how it would all come back to bite us on our backsides. Electric cars are now seen as the way ahead, in trying to keep our air clean. Back in the seventies British Leyland manufactured cars that guzzled petrol at an alarming rate. And all of those exhaust fumes only had one place to go. Not only were Austin Allegros ugly and uncomfortable, they also did their bit for drilling a big hole in the ozone layer.

THAT summer was all about knowing that when you went to bed, the next day was going to be just as warm and sticky as the previous one. Out of school for six weeks with nothing to worry about, was what the summer of 1976 was all about. It was my seventh summer, and it's one that I still think about today. At the time of writing these words, in August 2022, my part of the world is enjoying a particularly hot spell, which seems to show no signs of stopping. There has been no rain for weeks and there is none forecast in the foreseeable future. My lawn is a faded yellow and the earth is solid and cracked. I have just returned from Italy, where, although it was hot, it wasn't as hot as where I live. The heat is sapping and my nerves are sometimes frayed. When I was seven I didn't even think about the heat and I was never agitated. I was just a boy in a world of constant sunshine and good times. I suppose I must have thought once or twice that it would have been great if it could have gone on forever, but, as I learnt later on, nothing that makes us happy can be permanent. After the sunshine must come the rain. After the heat must come the cold. After the highs must come the lows.

An old dust-sheet, kept in the shed, was attached to our garden fence, with the other end being held up by a couple of wooden poles. And that was the summer tent which provided hours of amusement during the summer holidays. At lunchtime, sandwiches were the order of the day, filled with salad and cheddar cheese and Heinz salad cream. Orange squash was downed in great quantities and sometimes, after a trip to the local Pick-Your-Own fields, a punnet of strawberries would be carefully filled and paid for, to be eaten with sugar sprinkled on top and double cream poured over them. Dad would return from his morning shift at the factory, and he would be glad to sit in the shade for a few hours, watching as I made the most of those summer days. I didn't really need much to keep me amused, which is a trait that has stayed with me to this very day.

I occasionally ventured out of my tent, to walk the short distance to Victoria Park, where the swings and roundabouts waited for me. The message drummed into me, by my parents, was DON'T TALK TO STRANGERS. Their advice rang in my head like a dinging school-bell, and I always took care to avoid strange-looking men. To be fair, and as many people will testify, in the seventies there seemed to be a general air of innocence that blanketed those summer days. I'm not saying that paedophiles and abductors didn't exist – they certainly did – but they weren't as prolific in number as they are today. You could play at the park, and talk to strangers, knowing that most people were just there to enjoy themselves, and not wreak havoc. Mother, however, would sometimes accompany me to keep her eyes on me, although at times, when neither she or dad were free to supervise me, I'd take myself off alone to the park. I am talking about a time when mobile telephones didn't exist, so once I was out of the house, having fun, they had no idea what I was doing or where I was. Today, it is hard to imagine young children venturing out without a telephone in their possession.

Summer meant trips to Dreamland, that wonderful funfair overlooking Margate's sandy beach. We didn't own a car, so we took a train, which itself was always something to look forward to. Memories of those day-trips by train are still vivid in my mind, after the decades that have gently elapsed. We would walk from Margate railway station, through the town, towards the beach, hoping to find a spot that we could occupy for a couple of hours. Sandwiches had been made back at home, and were transported in plastic boxes, which were in a bag that dad carried with him. Buying food and drink on days out was really beyond my parents' means, so a picnic was always the order of the day. Dad had two weeks to relax every summer, away from the factory in which he spent most of his working life. His sole treat on those trips out would be a pint of beer, which he drank from a chunky glass. Needless to say I had the occasional sip of his beer, with its bitter taste putting me off the stuff for life – well, at least until I was sixteen.

After the beach came the funfair, with its diesel fumes and whirring and buzzing and ringing sounds being what all real funfairs were about. The most impressive ride was the roller-coaster, but that was always a no-no for a small lad like me, with asthma. I preferred the gentle and harmless fun of the ghost train and the dodgems. The rides were only ten pence a go, but back then that would have been a lot of money to my parents. After a few hours in the fair, we'd walk along the seafront, where, and even if the budget was going to explode, I'd be treated to a paper cone loaded with chips, and afterwards a ninety-nine ice cream. To this day I can still smell the vinegar on the chips, and feel the soft ice cream dripping down my chin. And all of these memories encased in summer days from yesteryear.

When dad's holiday was over, and mum had gone back to her own part-time job, I was still on holiday. Trips to Deal seafront would sometimes be a great way to kill a few hours. The beach was only a short walk from our house, which involved walking through three different alleyways. The DON'T TALK TO STRANGERS message was still fresh in my head, but those alleyways didn't scare me. I'd sometimes ride my bike to the seafront, with no respect for the law as I pedalled like a lunatic along the pavements and through the alleys. I'd sometimes get a dirty look from an old biddy, who admonished me for pedalling past her at breathtaking speed, and once or twice I was told to get off the pavement and stay on the road. I just laughed and pedalled on, unperturbed and in a hurry to get to the beach.

If Margate beach is sandy and wide, the beach at Deal is in complete contrast. There's not a grain of sand to be found on the narrow stretch of *plage,* where huge pebbles made it the least ideal place to lie down and relax. I still remember the sound of the waves raking the pebbles, and the fact that it was all too easy to sprain one's ankle as I carefully negotiated a passage to the water's edge. I'd have a paddle back then, because I couldn't swim and I was afraid of the water. On a hot summer's day the heat would have been unforgiving, but that grey-green seawater in which I plodded along was always cold and uninviting. I still remember fishing boats lined up on the beach, secured with rusty chains, with beautiful names like *Lady Dee* and *Angela.* The local fishermen must have named their boats after their loved ones. The beach is long, and sometimes I'd walk the length of it until I arrived at north Deal, where my uncle and auntie lived.

There is a golf course in north Deal, which hugs the coast and which was a great place to spend a few hours, once the excitement of the beach had worn away. Before you arrive at the first tee, there is a stretch of unloved land, full of bunkers, dying branches and empty beer cans. I'd zoom around here on my bicycle, negotiating an imaginary obstacle course. On a good day there would always be loads of kids riding around and having fun, in a time when we didn't even think of perverts and wrongdoers who perhaps wanted to harm us. I wasn't as hard as nails, but I really didn't let such thoughts enter my mind. Anyway, there were always a few parents around, who surveyed all of the children whilst not spoiling their fun. A visit to the golf course wouldn't have been complete without a ride past the first tee, which was always bound to upset some snobby golfers, who seemed to take life too seriously. Then, if I had the money to do so, I'd buy an ice lolly from the wooden shack at the entrance to the golf course. Other children with their parents would form an orderly queue, waiting to be served, as the waves crashed onto the beach and the warm air that filled the endless blue sky weighed heavy on our shoulders.

That's how summers should always be, I thought. I shouldn't have been ill, in bed, but outdoors enjoying myself in the fresh air. THAT'S the summer engraved in my mind – an indelible memory filed away with a few other golden memories. Sick, and then cured slowly and surely over the following years, until the bastard illness that had dragged me down was gone. Then outdoors all of the time, summer after summer, until school was done and dusted, and those long holidays became a thing of the past. Sparkling, carefree days like those from 1976 still entice me in moments of deep sleep, when the world is a less kinder place than it was. Like a drug that cures all maladies, nostalgia is potent and uplifting. It is a world that we knew, which we cannot return to, but it is a world we can look at, smile at and be happy that we were part of. As I write these words summer has just begun, the sky is a mix of heavy clouds and slats of blue. The world is aggressive and for some of us there are too many challenges to make life worth living. Today's children have their mobile telephones, tablets and whatever else people manufacture to keep us happy, but they don't have passion for the simple things in life.

A bike ride from the golf course back to my home was a

chance to see life and do what I wanted to do, in the way I wanted to do it. Pedalling like a madman possessed, away from those sandy dunes and the barren landscape, past the pub at the end of the road where my uncle and auntie lived, and past the timber yard. The gasometer to my left, which always impressed me with its size and the fact that it seemed to grow or shrink, always seemed to glimmer like a white diamond in the sunlight. Past the sweetshop, with its dirty windows and faded sign, around the bend – but carefully as I took it – and towards the level crossing. If I was lucky the barriers would be down, and I'd be forced to wait for a train to come into or leave Deal station. I'd wave at the driver, and sometimes he would wave back - a simple gesture of no importance, but something that made me feel good. Then it was over the crossing and past the bus depot to my right. I'd stop a while and study the dirty red buses, as their engines grumbled and spewed out fumes into the warm air. Buses that would come and go all day long, to places that were sometimes too far away for me to pedal my bicycle to. Then I'd be on my way again, for the final stretch home. Turn right, past the unfriendly-looking pub, negotiate the bend and finally home. Into the garden and under the old dust-sheet to calm down and cool down.

In a few weeks I would be back at school, back at the primary school in which I learnt the basic necessities to get through life. Reading, writing and counting, all of which I picked up quickly, without a great deal of effort. Some others would take longer, and others would learn quicker, but my peers were of no interest to me. If someone is more intelligent than me, then I've got no problem with that. If someone is richer than me, then that's fine. If someone is less intelligent than me, or poorer than me, then they must ask themselves why. Either way, what other people have or what other people are is of no interest to me. That's how it was when I was pedalling my bike along, under the golden sun, in 1976. It was just me being happy, not interested in other people. Just me, my rusty bicycle and no idea of where I was going.

Children back then were less aggressive than the children of today. You might have been a kid with wealthy parents, who bought you the latest computer for Christmas, but that didn't seem to inspire jealousy in other children. I had a friend like that, whose parents were financially comfortable. They bought him a Commodore Vic 20 and then a Commodore 64, when both machines were more or less released onto the market. He wasn't a flash kid, and he didn't mind me going round to his house on Saturday mornings to spend a few hours playing computer games with him. There was no goading or big-headiness, and he never got into any problems with his schoolmates because of his fortunate situation. Today a fifteen-year-old child is capable of stabbing a classmate because their telephone is better than his. And this is the world in which we live today. In 1976 you wouldn't have read about stabbings and gang attacks at schools. It was unheard of. Schools, back then, were places where we went to be educated. Today they are places where children go to, because they have no choice in the matter, with learning being the last thing on their minds.

3: Hard Times, Good Times.

It was in fact no bed of roses. It may have been bright and sunny throughout summer, but the harsh truth of the matter is that life at home wasn't always a walk in the park. But when you're a seven-year-old boy spending hot days in the garden, in a makeshift tent during the school holidays, and riding your bicycle along the seafront, you tend not to see the real aspects of life. You tend not to understand the struggles that go on behind the scenes, to keep a roof over your head and put food on the table. Money didn't fall from the sky, and it never will. Life was hard.

Dad – may he rest in peace – was what people call a *worker*. He wasn't idle, and he wasn't one for complaining if he didn't feel well. He just got on with going to work, at the factory in Sandwich where he would continue to work up until the time he was made redundant. He spent over thirty years of his life in a shit-hole making water bottles and other rubbery things. For over thirty years he'd trudge off to work, morning, afternoon and night, coming home at the end of the week with his weekly pay. Back then factory workers were paid in cash, on a weekly basis, and not paid a great deal. Whatever he earned was never enough, and whenever he brought his pay home he knew that.

But he had slipped into a routine that suited him, because working in a factory, although difficult and physically draining, was what appealed to him. He had been in the Royal Marines, and had lived in Singapore for a few years, and he had studied hard to be a drafts-man. He could have done great things with his life, because he had a gift and he was intelligent. But I don't think he wanted any responsibility, and he didn't want to set the world on fire. He left the Royal Marines and did a few jobs before slipping into the routine that he would adhere to for virtually the rest of his life. He had a wife and two young boys to support, his council-house rent to pay and food and clothes to buy. It was never going to be easy, but working at the factory didn't stress him out in any way. He always believed that everything was going to be okay, and tomorrow would always be better.

The money came in and went back out again. Saving money was a dream. My parents didn't have a telephone installed until I was almost eighteen and their first car came when I was at least thirty. That was what life was like back then for my family and millions of others. But even if money was thin on the ground, which it was permanently, my brother and I always had decent birthdays, Christmases and one holiday a year. We had a warm house in winter and a garden to play in, in summer. We had three square meals a day and on Friday nights we had a bag of sweets bought for us. We had a black and white television until it died, and my parents were forced to buy a colour one. We had comfortable furniture and bath night was once a week, always on a Sunday. My brother and I had our own bedrooms, because we lived in a three-bedroom council house, and we had two toilets. For years we had antiquated central heating, which the doctor said was one of the causes of my asthma. By the time my parents had bought their home from the council, and ripped out the central heating, I was well into my twenties.

Buying their home from Dover council was a massive step for them. If I remember rightly the purchase took place during the early eighties, when I was at still at school. The property cost them about ten thousand pounds, which back then would have been a lot of money for my parents. They managed to get an endowment mortgage and signed up for twenty-five years with the Leeds Building Society. At last they had a home of their own, thanks to Margaret Thatcher's scheme of allowing long-term council tenants the right to buy their house. This scheme has since been mocked by following generations, but it gave my parents the opportunity to put their feet on the property ladder.

Mum worked at the local Marks and Spencer, as a part-time shop assistant. We're talking about a time when Marks and Spencer was flying high, in a time before the High Street was reshaped and internet shopping took over our lives. One of her perks was the right to buy food that was always near to its sell by date, meaning that every Thursday evening she would return home with shopping bags loaded with goodies for all of the family. With hindsight I reckon she must have put a lot of her own wages back into her employer's till, but back then we didn't really care about that. Marks and Spencer used to, and still do, sell extraordinary food. Their trifles are the best to be had, and their cakes and sandwiches are just great. We didn't own a car, but we sometimes ate the best food money could buy.

Even with a mortgage around their necks, and with money still tight, my parents always took us away on holiday. We once went to the Isle of Wight, and then to Minehead, in Somerset, which my parents hired a car for. And then, when I was about fourteen, they decided to go on holiday to Spain. It was the first time my brother and I would be going abroad, which meant one-year visitor passports had to be applied for, and travellers cheques had to be saved up for. The excitement of standing in the check-in queue at Gatwick Airport is still fresh in my mind today. We seemed to have moved up a notch, and a few of my classmates were jealous of the fact that I had been to Spain for two weeks during the summer holidays. Back then, of course, package holidays were cheap and cheerful things, but still the money had to be found to pay for them. And the following year we went to Ibiza, for another sun-blessed fortnight. But still it didn't seem right. We were having holidays in the sun and my parents owned their own home, yet when the holidays were over dad would trudge off back to the factory, bring home his weekly pay and mother would seem to berate him.

My brother and I had to be fed and clothed. We grew quickly and last year's clothes suddenly became too small. We ate well and never went without. Christmastime seemed to be an orgy of good food and alcohol. I remember sipping snowballs and Babycham, whilst watching endless hours of Christmas television. The turkey came from Marks and Spencer and Christmas lunch was always a magnificent affair. Back then it was probably my preferred part of the year, because it seemed to comfort me. Only good things came out of Christmas. It was like the summer of 1976, stuck on to the end of every year. Today I loathe Christmas and all that it stands for. When I think of the money my parents must have spent every year, just to celebrate a few days in December, it all seems so ridiculous. But when you're a child, surrounded by Christmas trees and mince pies, you see things differently.

I think all children bring shame upon their parents, at one time or another. I did so when I was caught shoplifting from the sweetshop opposite my primary school. I had been stealing for a few weeks when the shopkeeper finally caught me. He said that he would have to tell my mother, who always went into the shop on a Friday evening to buy my brother and I a bag of sweets. I think I was caught on a Tuesday afternoon, and the wait until Friday seemed to go on forever. Needless to say, come Friday, my mother tore me to shreds. However, it wasn't for the fact that I had been caught, but more about what the shop-keeper would think of her. Dad gave me a semi-bollocking, which was no surprise. Although he knew it was morally wrong to steal, he realised that all young boys shoplifted at some stage of their lives.

And then the summer of 1976 evaporated, and was never to be seen again. The following summers were miserable affairs, and the winters became harsher. Asthma still affected me, and life at home was changing with the times. Mother once brought a ready-meal home from Marks and Spencer. It was duck à l'orange, which is basically roast duck cooked with oranges, and usually served with peas. Dad didn't approve of foreign muck buggering up his menu. Monday nights were reserved for egg and chips. Duck never made a reappearance in the house again.

My time at primary school was coming to an end. I was glad to be leaving the bastard place, but I wasn't that happy about having to continue my education at Deal Secondary School. My brother, being six years older than me, had blazed a trail and had finished his schooling with glowing grades. He had set the bar very high. I would never emulate his achievements in the classroom, because I was lazy and I got bored very quickly. The pressure was always going to be on me. But competition like that didn't interest me. He would do things his way, and I would do things my way.

The seventies were just over when I finished the first part of my education. Britain was evolving. Dad was still at the factory and mother still at Marks and Spencer. Margaret Thatcher had just started the beginning of her eleven-year reign. Dad hated Thatcher. He was a working-class man, and she didn't have any time for him. He would however buy his council house thanks to her initiative. The boom and bust economy was about to take off, and opportunities galore would soon manifest. And I still think that if I had been born ten years earlier I would have grabbed the opportunities by the throat. But we're born when we are born, and we must make do with what we have. Nothing can change that, and nothing can change the fact that we are obliged to go to school before we go to work.

My short-wearing days were over. A change of school meant a change of uniform, including long trousers. Trudging to school in the future winter months would now be less of an endurance. At least I would have warm legs. But school uniforms cost money that my parents didn't really have. A pair of long trousers, grey shirts, a pullover and a tie, with the school's crest and motto printed on it, all had to be bought. I was dragged to the shop to try on various shirts and trousers until we found the ones that fitted me. And that's when the penny dropped. It was just before the new term, in 1980. A new decade meant a new school. All that carefree fun that I had enjoyed in the seventies suddenly seemed like a distant memory. As the school holidays came to an end I started to feel less excited about the forthcoming changes in my life. I had loathed my primary school, and I had a feeling that my next school wasn't going to be a lot better. The last few days of the holiday shot by, until the final weekend crept up on me. And then what had really been an age of innocence was over.

4: School - 1980.

At the time of writing this chapter it is winter. The sharp and violent below-zero air temperature has left the lawn frozen. Yet in the sunny side of the garden the grass is lush and green, having pushed up gradually during what, up to now, has been a very mild winter. I haven't felt a single snowflake on my face in Normandy, where I have lived for almost twenty years. The wind has sometimes bitten into me, and some mornings, like this morning, have been harsh. But winter in the snow-up-to-your-ankles sense of the word is absent.

The ritual back then was always the same. I'd pull back the curtains in January and see an even sheet of snow covering the back garden. But if in my young mind I was hoping to get out of going to school, I had been wishing for the impossible. Deal Secondary School was a fifteen-minute walk away, but through the ankle-deep snow it was almost double that. Surely my parents wouldn't want to send their youngest son out in THAT? I went downstairs, still dressed in my pyjamas, hoping for a quiet day indoors playing with my Lego. When father told me to get back upstairs and get changed for school, my plans were immediately shelved. The Lego would have to wait until my day at school was done. I returned a few moments later dressed in my school attire. I looked out of the dining room window. Flakes as big as lumps of coal were coming down thick and fast. My big winter coat would be the only protection I'd have to keep me warm, as I set out on my journey to that bastard school. But before I contemplated by epic journey to there, a hot breakfast was the order of the day.

I fucking hate porridge. The last time I ate it – forced to do so, because it would apparently keep me warm throughout the day – was on those winter mornings, before setting off for school. Mother would prepare it in the kitchen, on the small gas stove, and then she'd bring the saucepan through to the dining room, where massive dollops of the stuff were shovelled into my bowl. On some mornings she hadn't properly mixed the dry flakes with the hot milk, but any complaints were soon rejected. She never once told me to eat it and shut the fuck up, but her reply always conveyed the same message. The congealed foodstuff was made marginally more edible by adding some Tate & Lyle sugar, which was kept in a glass dish with a teaspoon permanently stuck in it. The sugar would melt and leave a sweet layer of crystals on the surface of the porridge. Then would come a mug of tea, piping hot, served with the warning that I had to get a move on if I wasn't to be late for school. Another glance out of the window depressed me even further. The snow was piling up nicely, and my shiny shoes wouldn't be able to resist the icy-cold snow from penetrating them. Great, I thought, as I anticipated another day of wearing soaking socks, before I left the house protected to the eyeballs with a hood, scarf and gloves.

Those annual winter treks were always hard, especially as the sky never seemed to change from its menacing grey colour throughout the day, and the cold air left you feeling sapped of all energy. The winters of today are different, and today's generation is less hardy than the previous one. Some people now don't go to work, and don't send their kids to school, if there a centimetre-thick layer of snow on the ground. They just don't want to go outside in the cold and icy conditions, telling themselves that their employer will understand and that the school is probably shut anyway. But back then we had four clear seasons, and some winters were particularly severe. But never once was I allowed to stay at home, to avoid getting wet feet, and never once did my parents not go to work. I had to go to school, because education was important. People had to go to work, because money was already tight, and it didn't grow on trees.

I made it to school, and my feet were freezing. There were a few cars in the car park, which meant that some of the teachers were there. Some kids milled around at the entrance, hoping that there would be no lessons for today. I hated that school with a passion, and on those miserable winter mornings my hatred was intensified. Its cold corridors smelt of decay in those freezing months, and the classrooms were full of kids shivering because of the inadequate heating. The floor was slippery and dangerous, where snow had been trod in and brought into the building under our leaking shoes. A lot of kids were absent, being kept at home by sympathetic parents. After all, a few days off in the five years they would be at Deal Secondary School wouldn't have much of an impact on their education, would it? Sometimes we would have our lessons, and the teacher giving it wouldn't be the usual one, due to staff absences. You could see that the teacher couldn't give a fuck, and was just going through the motions, wishing that he or she was back at home, sat in front of the television and drinking hot chocolate. The bastard headmaster was a terrible man. He surveyed the kids as they trickled in, making sure that they resisted the temptation of having snowball fights. Some kids trudged through the snow, on the playing fields, and were duly admonished for their stupidity. But none of them cared, because the headmaster was a wanker, and their time at his school wouldn't last forever.

I always tried to keep my nose clean during those five long years, but it was a continual struggle. I had the inevitable scrapes with other kids, and some teachers preferred me to others. There was no social media back in those days, but everyone in Deal knew that Deal Secondary School was a shambles. I was in the upper band, which meant I should have done well, but I think that it was all wasted on me. If I could have stayed at home and played with my Lego all day, I don't believe I would have turned out any worse. I learnt a few things, and excelled in a couple of subjects, but I was never going to set the world on fire. I had an older brother, who had passed through the same school a few years before me, and he had always done very well, with his top-of-the-class performances. So there was already pressure on me to emulate him, but I never lived up to his academical standards. I was no match for him, but I could have been if I had applied myself.

Some winters seemed to drag on for months and months. The days sitting in those freezing classrooms were never-ending. Often I would get to the school gates, after my thirty-minute hike, and find out that the heating had packed up. There was no school today, so I had to turn around and go back home. On the return journey we'd be even colder and more miserable, but we'd have a snowball fight on the fields and just piss around in the snow. The sun wouldn't make an appearance for days on end, and when it finally did the slow thaw would begin, and the snow and ice would transform into rivers of slush. But still the porridge came, and still I was pushed out of the door and told to go to school. Then the slush would disappear, leaving the playing fields looking like something out of the Somme, after another bloody battle in the trenches. And the kids would walk through that mud, just like me, and just like me they would be collared by the headmaster, and made to pick up all the rubbish from the fields, just to teach us a lesson.

Five years is a long time to not enjoy something. But if you tweaked a few knobs, prepared yourself mentally and told yourself that the end was in sight, it was easier to get through the ordeal. Those porridge-fuelled mornings served me well, even though I couldn't see it back then. I mean, how did those kids turn out who were kept at home by their parents, in those harshest of winters? Are they now parents, in their mid-fifties, who mollycoddle their own children? Did they become anything? I work with young people today, and I sometimes think that if they had been around with me, when I was as school, they wouldn't have lasted ten minutes. I just want to shake them up and give them a boot up the backside. Those winter months from long ago are etched into my mind. I remember when I got home from school and yanked off my shoes. My socks would be soaking wet, and I couldn't feel my toes. My shoes leaked, but because money was tight there was never the chance of replacing them. They only got replaced when my feet got bigger. And I had to polish those shoes once a week, and I had to take care of my duffel coat. Kids were sometimes nasty back then, but it was a nastiness on a lower level. There were no knives and death threats, but perhaps a scuffle after school. But there was never the kind of violence that we see today. I hated some of my teachers, but I wouldn't have entertained the idea of stabbing them with a kitchen knife. I hated that wanker of a headmaster, who seemed to have it in for me from day one, but I knew that he wouldn't always be on my back.

The old school has since been demolished, and replaced by a better and brighter model. Some nights I think about those winter-morning starts, and have flashbacks of me trudging through the snowy streets. You can pull any building down, but the memories of it will always remain. Apart from those winter episodes, the first day I was there was the worse. And, as for most kids, the final day was the best. Those teachers who were supposed to teach me were, on reflection, totally useless. The headmaster, now deceased, was a vindictive bastard. His assistant was another strange one, in his tiny office at the end of the corridor. Many a time I was summonsed to see him, or my parents were invited to hear about my erratic behaviour. Everyone scratched their heads, because the general consensus was that I had the ability to do well. The trouble is that you can't get someone to excel if they're not motivated. And how did they motivate people back then? Well, they didn't. That school was no worse than a factory, with new faces and old fodder passing through every day. And anyway, jobs back then were easy to get, with or without qualifications. You could pick a job like picking apples off a tree. There were enough to go round, and if you didn't like what you were doing, you could always find something else to do.

I was regularly punished for my crimes. Once, my French class went on a day trip to Calais, but I was left behind because of my poor behaviour. That punishment, I must admit, hurt me. I had been looking forward to seeing what life was like on the other side of the Channel. My parents had stumped up the money for the trip, which wasn't easy considering their precarious financial situation. But the ferry left without me. I lied and told my parents that the trip had been cancelled, and that they would get a refund, which they duly did. I then feigned illness on the day of the trip, as there was no school for me that day. My auntie told my mother that she had seen my classmates getting off the coach, at the school, after their trip. They were all clutching baguettes. My mother was confused. I just shrugged it off and said that it must have been another class.

Feigning illness also got me out of going swimming at another local school's pool. I must have been ill at least twenty times during one year. The other kids loved splashing around in the freezing water, but I was better suited to watching from the sidelines. What sort of draconian system forces children to go swimming in an open-air pool, if they don't want to do it? It's the same system that makes severely asthmatic children like me run two miles around a massive field, once a week, in the name of physical exercise. I was usually coughing up my guts at the end of the run, with my games teacher – a fine man, who sadly died of a brain tumour – congratulating me on my effort. He knew that I was never going to be the next Steve Ovett, but he admired my courage. He was a good teacher, who I always got on with.

And that's all that was needed – teachers with a kind word and a helping hand. If she who took the swimming classes had been more humane, instead of being a most vile individual, I would have gladly splashed around in the water. If he who taught me maths hadn't bawled and screamed at me, because I was talking to my neighbour instead of paying attention, I might have come to respect him more. If she who taught me physics hadn't stunk of stale body odour, I might have become a nuclear scientist. If he who taught me French had been more dynamic and interesting, I might have spoken the language. I excelled at English and Geography, because I got on well with my teachers.

And what did those five years give me? Well, I was on holiday when my 'O' Level results plopped through the letterbox. My psychic skills told me that it wasn't even worth opening the envelope – but I did because my mother was standing behind me. They had been five wasted years, with only a grade D in English and grade C in Geography to crow about. I stared at the slip of paper and told myself that everything was going to be fine. Mother shouted at me, and father, when he came in from work, just looked at her and said

I'd probably be okay. Then they rowed about me and my future. Mother always worried. Father didn't. Mother was wrong. Father was right.

All I wanted then was to be on the road to employment. Secondary school had been a terrible place, like an open prison where you're allowed to leave for lunch, but you had to go back in the afternoon. That bastard establishment, with its bastard teachers, was more of a hindrance to me, than a help. I can't honestly think of one thing I learnt there that was of use to me. I had no mind for physics, chemistry or history, and even less for maths and religious studies. It was like turning up at a factory, doing your stint and then going home. Most people who work in factories have no interest in what they're manufacturing, and don't understand why they're making what they make. They just turn up for the money and a few weeks paid holiday. They learn nothing. If I could find a job, I thought, that would prove that education is basically an overrated waste of time. If I could find a job, I thought, I could set out my stall and do things my way.

And so, at sixteen, my school days were over. The shackles were off. Never again would I have to trudge through snow, early in the morning. Never again would a teacher throw a board rubber at me. Never again would I sit through a biology lesson. But I would have to do something, if I was to appease mother. I spent those first few weeks of early summer considering my options. I felt confident that I could make something of my life, but with only two 'O' Levels it was going to be harder than I would have liked. And then I found the solution.

5: Y.T.S. Boy – 1985.

I didn't want to do it, but I had no choice in the matter. It was a case of either go to college or   join one of the Y.T.S.'s, hoping that after a year-long period of learning and training I'd come out of it all with a decent job. The idea of going to college had never appealed to me, as I considered furthering one's education a waste of time. So the Y.T.S. it was to be, with me deciding that my future was going to be in computing and information technology. The opportunities at the time were endless, so I was fairly convinced that I'd come out of it all smiling.

The Youth Training Scheme, for those unfamiliar with the concept, was a government-run training scheme in which sixteen-year-olds would spend a year with an approved employer, learning the aspects of a particular trade. There would be a need to attend college once a week, to study the subject in more detail, with a view of hoping to get a qualification at the end of the year-long course. The pay was, if I recall correctly, £26.00 per week, which was paid by the employer. If I kept my nose clean, and my head down, I could come out of the year-long training period with a good job with the employer, or at least experience in my preferred field. In the 1980's information technology was taking off big time in Britain, so I felt fairly certain that I'd do okay.

Sandwich, a quaint English town just a few miles from my hometown, was where Pfizer, the global pharmaceuticals giant, had a massive research centre and production plant. It employed thousands of people, and was by far the largest employer in the area. Its site at the edge of Sandwich was a sprawling complex of offices, laboratories and production facilities, where, amongst other things, they would eventually develop and make Viagra. If I could get my feet in the door here, I thought, I might end up getting a job for life. And so dressed in my best grey suit and grey, plastic shoes, I got a train to Sandwich, and walked from the station to where I would eventually spend the first year of my after-school life. Thinking back, I must have looked like a pimp in my appalling suit and shiny shoes, but my interviewer must have been impressed, because a few days later I got the call saying I had been offered a place in Pfizer's I.T. department.

Pfizer had it all. They ran a bus service for its employees, with lots of buses picking up the company's personnel from all over that part of Kent. My pick-up point was just outside Sholden church, where I boarded the bus at eight o'clock every morning. I've never suffered with first-day nerves in any job I've had, so this New Boy in his favourite suit and shoes just looked out of the window, as happy as the circumstances allowed me to be, as the bus weaved its way to its final destination. It was only then, when we had arrived at the site, that the size of it all left me in awe. Then the stench hit my nostrils – a rich, stifling odour that seemed to hang in the air, being pumped out of chimneys in huge clouds of vapour.

I think there were about twenty of us on that first day, and we were ushered into a huge room, where we sat and listened attentively as our trainers – two kind-hearted people, if I remember correctly – told us what to expect from our year's training course with Pfizer. Then, once we had all stood up for five minutes, to introduce ourselves to our fellow trainees, we were taken on a tour of the site. The office complex was a sprawling concern, with offices scattered over several floors. Individual workstations, separated by orange dividers were everywhere, and there seemed to be an air of stuffiness wafting through the place. Pretty girls were photocopying reams of documents and distributing pages of computer printouts. There was a sort of deathly silence running through the corridors, only broken by the sound of the tea ladies wheeling their trolleys along, going into each of the offices asking if anyone wanted a cup of tea or coffee. A visit to the production facility followed, where drugs were concocted and knocked out by huge, noisy machines. The smell coming from huge vats was overwhelming, and everywhere you looked there were employees taking readings and overseeing the production process. These were interesting times for the company, as the research and development of Viagra was ongoing, with it eventually being manufactured at the site in the following decade. The tour ended with a visit to the company's restaurant, which served hundreds of meals everyday. The food, I can confirm, was excellent, with a menu that changed on a regular basis. I thought, as I looked at the hundreds of happy employees enjoying their lunches, that Pfizer would be a great place to work.

After two weeks I was bored rigid. Computers were never going to turn me on, and were never going to be the foundations on which I was going to build my professional life. The mainframes were noisy, bulky bastards, and I had the task of replacing the back-up tapes once a day. What a tedious task that was to become. Huge reels, the size of bus steering wheels, had to be pushed along on a trolley, and loaded into the mainframes in a specified order. Then, after pushing a few buttons, the spools would turn merrily around, recording data for posterity. Then pages upon pages of data would be printed out, and placed in pigeon holes all over the site, so the relevant people could analyse the data and see if everything was going to plan. And that, during fifty-two weeks, was all that I did.

Some people were okay, and others smelt of stale body odour. Reg was a kind-hearted man, but I knew that he had no interest in explaining things to me. He wore the same shirt all week, and come Friday the smell coming from his armpits was enough to have me keeping a safe distance from him. He used to get me to do his photocopying for him – a task which involved copying at least five hundred pages of numbers and mathematical equations. The photocopiers broke down on a regular basis, mainly because I pushed them to their limits. Secretaries would come and smile, and help me unblock the wretched machines, asking me if I was enjoying myself. How the hell anyone could get pleasure from doing such a mundane task was beyond me, but I just smiled back and made all the right noises.

In moments of intense boredom, of which there were many, I'd wonder off along the corridors, walking in and out of offices just to see what was going on. On each floor there was an area with potted plants and coffee machines, and I'd spend half an hour drinking sweet hot chocolate whilst gazing out of the huge windows that gave a view onto the massive company car park. Thousands of people worked at the site, and come lunchtime it seemed like they all congregated in the company restaurant at the same time. To be honest, the food was good, and for me it was free. Chips with everything was my lunchtime fodder, before I returned to my photocopying and tape-loading duties.

My days finished at five o'clock, and by then I was glad to get on the bus and get back home. My cheap suit was uncomfortable and my plastic shoes pinched my toes. The thought of going back to the site the next day left me feeling depressed and unmotivated, and my time at Pfizer turned out to be a very unproductive one. A year wasted, is how I see it, working in an environment that wasn't suited to me. Some of my fellow trainees ended up getting employed by the company, but I suppose that my lack of interest showed, and so no job offers came my way. Mondays to Thursdays were sheer hell, with only Fridays bringing me some much-needed relief. I would have given up on the course before the end of the year, but that would have meant complications in getting unemployment benefit. Instead, and like a good photocopying and tape-loading trainee, I saw my time out, collecting my £26.00 pay cheque every Friday.

When the end eventually came it was with a pop, instead of a bang. My trainers had written a report on me, and it didn't make pleasant reading: "Doesn't seek to get involved and happy just to do the most basic of tasks." It seemed like a prolongation of my school days, at the end of which my teachers had written an equally damning assessment of me. To hell with Pfizer and to hell with the people who had dared to write such unjustifiable things about me. Keeping the reference served no purpose, as a potential employer wouldn't be impressed by what had been written about me. So it went into the bin, in which I had also planned to throw my plastic shoes and ill-fitting suit. But I was now technically unemployed, so the suit and shoes would be needed to dazzle someone into giving me a job. And, as it would happen, that job would come quicker than I had imagined.

But I wasn't going to rush into anything. Choosing the right job was like planning a move in a game of chess. It had to be thought through, with all the potential consequences of the move needing to be considered. Her Majesty's government was now paying me unemployment benefit, which was enough to pay for a few pints and a weekly driving lesson. Some people don't like being unemployed, because they think that there is a stigma attached to receiving handouts. Personally, I believe that being unemployed is nothing to be ashamed of. It's just a way of life, that many people will have to deal with one day or another. Some people plunge into depths of depression when they lose their jobs, and others, like myself, just see it as another chapter in their lives. You just need to stay positive and wait for the right opportunity to present itself. I enjoyed a few moths of glorious idleness, but I soon became bored. Drinking pints at lunchtime was okay for a while, but once the novelty had worn off, it was time to get into the world of active employment.

6: A Real Job – 1986.

The Job Centre, in Deal, became a regular part of my life once my time at Pfizer was done. Some young men of my age were happy to piss their dole money up the wall, drinking in one of the town's numerous pubs, but I was not like them. I wanted to go to work, get financial independence, move out of my childhood home and move into a flat of my own. Big plans for a seventeen-year-old lad who had two 'O' Levels and nothing else. But I had drive and I was determined to get that first job as soon as I could. After all, this was a time when jobs were to be had, if you didn't mind turning your hand to anything. Formal qualifications helped, but the right attitude was probably just as important. It also helped if you were mobile, which is why I was in the middle of learning to drive.

Job details were printed on cards, which were arranged in racks under various headings. There were manual jobs, jobs in shops, office jobs, jobs in catering, there was always a demand for taxi drivers, bar staff and restaurant waiters. Some jobs required no experience and others required a bucket-load of 'O' Levels. Some jobs were far away and others were closer to home. Some jobs paid well and others didn't. There were apprenticeships and training courses. There were part-time jobs and jobs that filled forty hours in a week. Either way, there was usually something for someone, or perhaps nothing for everyone. It just didn't pay to be fussy or difficult.

One job I went for was that of cloakroom assistant at a local bingo club in Dover. No former experience was required, which seemed right because looking after some old biddy's coat whilst she went to play bingo was hardly rocket science. The pay was as to be expected and the hours were in line with a bingo club. The job had my name written all over it, but sadly it wasn't to be. The manageress told me that they were looking for someone with at least some experience. What a waste of fucking time and train fare that turned out to be. I didn't do much better at my local branch of Currys, where, apparently, selling radio-cassette players required previous retail experience and more than two 'O' Levels. I never bought anything from that shop from that day on. My efforts to become a stock controller at a local metalworks also came to nothing, as did my attempt to become an assistant at a car-rental company in Dover. MFI didn't even reply to my application and Tesco clearly had better people lined up to stack their shelves.

And then, after a few months of going round in circles, and travelling by train to numerous interviews, I got myself a job as a manifest clerk at a shipping company in Dover. The guy that interviewed me looked like Captain Birdseye, with his white beard, and he knew a good thing when he saw it. And he was honest. The pay, he said, wasn't much, and the working hours were not fantastic either. But sat there, dressed in my shiny suit, I just nodded my head and gave all the right replies. It turned out that he was the director, and when I told him I'd be interested in taking the job, he told me that the company owner would take me to see my new place of work, so that I'd know how to find it the following Monday morning, when I was going to start a week's trial. And with that the company owner appeared, before whisking me off in an oversized Mercedes, bearing a private registration number. He was a right flash bastard, and when I heard him talk to his employees, each sentence that spewed from his mouth was littered with every swear-word you could imagine. If he wasn't effing and blinding, he was clearly having a bad day.

And so began a two-year adventure, which played out in a cramped office in the corner of Dover Hoverport. I soon ditched my suit for jeans and a t-shirt, and the other guys made me feel welcome. The job involved typing freight manifests onto official forms, using a shitty old typewriter that had seen better days. If people arrived from the continent with undeclared freight – which could range from a piano to a crate of car parts – it was our job to take care of all of the paperwork, before lodging it with Customs and Excise, at their office just a short moped ride from our own office. And once Customs had cleared the paperwork their end, they stamped a little card, telling us that we could release the freight from a small holding compound, which looked like Arthur Daley's lock-up.

In summer it was a great job, because we were often outside commuting between our office, the compound and the office where we had to take the paperwork to. Tootling along on the company moped, which was falling apart and later upgraded for a more reliable model, was all part of the fun, as was wondering around the Hoverport late at night, when it was closed. In winter it was the worst of jobs imaginable, with rain lashing in from the English Channel and the moped ride becoming a feat of endurance. But when you're seventeen, and without a care in the world, such problems never really entered one's mind. My only problem back then was that I had failed my driving test twice, and was having to use trains to get to and from work. Apart from the fact that this was hardly an ideal way to get to work for six o'clock in the morning, it was also expensive. I therefore had no choice than to dodge paying the fare, whenever I could. I'm ashamed to admit that I probably cost British Rail a few hundred pounds during the time of my first job, but considering that the trains were filthy, and sometimes late, I told myself that it was only right that I didn't pay for such a shoddy service. My problem was later resolved when I passed my driving test at the third attempt, and I bought myself a bright orange Fiat.

It's true that the pay wasn't great, but it was more than the £26.00 I had been earning every week at Pfizer. My monthly pay at the start was £240.00, and at Christmastime we were given a £30.00 voucher for Dewhurst, the butchers, which I always gave to mother. It was thanks to this that we had a decent turkey to look forward to on Christmas day, which for once didn't come from Marks and Spencer. for the following two years. Other perks came from our clients, and ranged from a cake that someone's wife had made me for my birthday, to bottles of whisky or crates of beer that various truck drivers gave us. I always gave dad the whisky, because back then I hadn't yet become accustomed to the stuff. And I suppose the best perk came when I turned eighteen. It was then that my boss wangled me a free return trip to Calais, which included the chance to ride in the hovercraft's cockpit. It all seems so trivial now, but back then it was as best as I could have wanted.

People are what make jobs interesting, whether it be the people you work with or the people you serve. My colleagues were a good bunch, and even if they had a couldn't-care-less attitude, because of the size of their pay packet, they still did their job. We had a small yet comfortable office, and with the arrival of a new office manager, we later had a television, proper tea and coffee making facilities and an upgraded heating system, because in winter it was bloody freezing. We had one girl who worked with us, and I remember quite clearly that she had the biggest pair of breasts imaginable. She was eighteen, and said that her boyfriend had paid for her to have breast enhancement surgery. In summertime she came to work in tight shorts and even tighter t-shirts. She raised male blood pressures wherever she walked, wiggling her little backside as she walked along. She wasn't the sharpest knife in the draw, but sometimes intelligence isn't the most important attribute that a girl can have.

The new office manager was an ex-army major, who was looking to earn a bit of spare cash in his retirement. He lived in a nice house and drove a fancy car, and he certainly wasn't on his uppers, so I never understood why he would want to work for such a company. And HE was a character, who told us tales about his time in the army. Tall and slim, he marched at a rapid pace, when most of us just walked, and he brought some much-needed organisation to the office. In no time it was functioning with military precision, with daily updates on anything we needed to know being given on A4-sized sheets, which were pinned to a notice board. At lunchtime he drove home, and when he returned an hour later he stank of whisky. He was also a heavy smoker, and because he earned more than his staff, and was a generous man, he had no qualms in giving us the occasional cigarette – a gesture which he never expected to be repaid.

But as kind-hearted as he was, he also had a very nasty streak running through him. One young lad who came to work for us was clearly not up to the job. Unable to do the work required of him, the retired major just ground the poor bastard down until the lad was a quivering wreck. He would shout and scream at him, and belittle him in front of all of us. Of course, it was an unpleasant experience for the employee concerned, but for the rest of us it was real entertainment. It made me wonder just how the major had treated his own men, in the army. I imagined that he had probably been a complete and utter bastard.

When I turned eighteen the major secured me a pay rise. He told the company owner that I merited a substantial rise. In turn my pay went from £240.00 a month to £320.00. Big times, I thought. And the increase was more than welcome, because by then, and after passing my driving test at the third attempt, I had bought my first car. And so I was now fully mobile, driving around in a bright orange Fiat Scudo. That was one hell of a car, which had the acceleration of a tank and weighed just as heavy as one. But it was my first set of wheels. Sadly, the car and I didn't enjoy a lengthy relationship together, because it often broke down and rust had set in. I think it just died a death outside of my parents house, and had to be towed away to a scrapyard.

And when the car died I had to go back to getting the train to work. And that's when I decided that my time at the hoverport was probably coming to an end. It had been a fun experience, but it was never going to be a long-term number. The pay wasn't really any good, because the more I earned the more I would spend. I needed to find a job that paid better and had some sort of opportunities for me to advance. The major understood, and told me that there would always be a place for me if I wanted to return at a later date. I thanked him, but I didn't envisage returning. I had got myself a new job, with better pay, and for me the only was was up – or so I thought.

7: A New Britain.

Margaret Thatcher swept to power in 1979, on the back of a broken Britain, ruined by a devastating economical situation, blighted by industrial action and still living in the shadows of power cuts and shortened working weeks. Anything that she could do would surely be an improvement on what the British people were then enduring. Anything that her government could do would certainly help lift Britain out of the shit-filled pit in which it found itself.

And this is probably why the eighties are viewed as a boom period for Britain, and Thatcher is considered, alongside Churchill, as being Britain's finest prime minister. But looking back to the golden period, four decades ago, we now understand that it was all too good to be true, and that with smoke and mirrors Thatcher managed to run Britain for eleven years, until she finally came unstuck. By then, in November 1990, the damage had already been done. There had been boom years, that is for certain, but there had been periods of hardship which, despite all of her magic, she couldn't change.

My parents had taken advantage of the right-to-buy scheme, which allowed council tenants to buy their council houses, at a price cheaper than the current market value. This made my parents proud home-owners, and at last they could set about changing their end-of-terrace house into something that resembled a non-council house. Out went the archaic kitchen, windows and central heating system, and in came a modern eighties kitchen, double glazing and gas-powered radiators. Dad's wages hadn't really gone up in that period, and so the monthly mortgage repayment was often hard to find. The building society had given them an endowment mortgage, which, as we all know now, was just one of the biggest rip-offs that the banks had devised. Years later my parents, like thousands of other people throughout Britain, would later be compensated by their bank for the shoddy and tacky product which they had been sold with their mortgage. But at the time no-one thought for one moment that something was wrong, because people were borrowing heavily, buying houses, and in turn pushing up property values. Everything was rosy in the garden when one had a job to go to, but when the scourge of unemployment swept through Thatcher's green and pleasant land, things started to go wrong.

Apart from banks flogging dodgy mortgages, and creaming off commissions from the endowment providers, estate agents were having a hell of a time. Up, up, and away went house prices, leaving well-dressed estate agents to earn higher commissions for themselves. Viewed as unscrupulous and odious, they had joined the league of charlatans, in which they were jostling for top spot with financial advisers and second-hand car salesmen. And all of this was endorsed by Thatcher, who was all for free enterprise and earning a quick pound. Those other wonderful Thatcherite creations, yuppies, were earning millions off the back of the stock market, buying and selling in the week, before returning to their mock-tudor houses in Essex for the weekend. It was champagne and caviar all round, for them, as London and the home counties revelled in the boom times.

But in the north of Britain Thatcher was hardly seen as a saviour, if she was ever seen at all. For if the industrial heartland had once once powered the nation, and provided millions of jobs, it was a long way away from Basildon, and Thatcher's comfort zone. She was, quite rightly, despised by the very working-class people who she chose to ignore, creating a north-south divide which still exists to this very day. Closed factories went to ruin, industry died and the region suffered from a massive lack of investment. Millions of people from Liverpool to Newcastle became used to waiting for their dole money to arrive, knowing that there was no good news on the horizon. The Liverpool riots of 1981, when unemployment was soaring and the economy was suffering, were born from this very bleak and troubled period. The message was clear.

Yet still Thatcher went on the rampage against the old industries and the old way of doing things. She had no time for what she considered to be labour-intensive, state-run concerns. She had no interest in British Rail, which once had been the model of a state-run railway, throughout the world. Dogged by industrial action and poor management, Thatcher had toyed with the idea of privatising what was a considerable thorn in her side. Although British Rail remained state-run throughout her decade in power, it was her successor, John Major, who finally brought the axe down on it, when it was eventually broken up and sold off in 1984. At the time of writing Britain's railway infrastructure is a total shambles, with different train operating companies running the nation's rail network. If you thought British Rail was bad, it was actually very good indeed compared to today's chaos and disaster.

Old King Coal was another albatross around the government's neck which Thatcher wanted to rid herself of. Coal was now old hat, she considered, and so a massive plan was instigated to close Britain's mines and put thousands of miners on the dole. They would, she announced, receive generous redundancy packages and get help in training for a new career. The trouble for

Thatcher was that those men who had spent years working in the mines, in unsafe and unhealthy conditions, had no desire to retrain for a new career. Mining was in their blood. It was all they knew. Step up their leader, Arthur Scargill, who, as an ex-miner himself, understood his mens' passion and pride. There would be no closures and no redundancy packages. Scargill made that clear, and in doing so started a year-long bloody and bitter struggle against Thatcher.

That strike of 1984-1985 pushed Thatcher to her limits. Scargill literally lead his army into battles against the police, where violence overspilled and both sides fought bitterly to the very end. I remember watching the news reports on the strike, and it made grim viewing. And all of this was happening in Thatcher's promised land. The dispute lasted almost a year, and it was only when some of the miners started to return to work did the resistance start to ebb away. The damage caused was immense. I lived near to one of the Kent coal mines, and saw for myself the tragic side effects of the struggle. The scabs (those miners who had decided to return to work) were singled out by their striking colleagues. In my home town one man killed himself after succumbing to the constant stream of abuse aimed at him. In the end families were divided, and colleagues became outcasts. And it was all in vain. The industry as it was would eventually be consigned to history. It was a victory for Thatcher, but her armour had been seriously dented. Whole communities were blighted by unemployment and lives were ruined forever. And all of this because Thatcher considered coal to be outdated, dirty and uneconomical to mine. So today, four decades later, as Britain is going through an alarming energy crisis, deep in the ground there are thousands of tonnes of coal which, even if a dirty fuel, is much needed right now.

Rich or poor was the best way to describe British people during the eighties. The south-east of England was the golden triangle, where the affluent lived and where the Essex-boy culture was born. Vulgar, brash and bling-bling, living off the back of the good times was life for them. And when Thatcher started her programme of privatisation, the average man in the street wanted a piece of the action. British Gas, British Telecom and British Petroleum, to name a few, were all sold off, and the money received from the proceeds was used to prop up the ailing economy. Now these companies were owned by investors and financial giants. Thatcher had sold the family silver, but those Essex boys were raking in a fortune. But the further north of London you went, that golden triangle seemed like another land. There were no Essex boys in Liverpool and Newcastle, but just poor souls who had been overlooked and abandoned by Thatcher and her government.

The conflict to take back control of the Falkland Islands was Thatcher's career-saving moment. Struggling in the polls, with the economy on the ropes, victory over the Argentine aggressors would see that her mandate to govern would be extended. 1982 would be a pivotal time for her. She saved her skin and indeed never looked back. But things would have ended differently if Argentina or Scargill had come out on top, and Thatcher knew that. And so on she went, driving home the message that Britain was booming, and that if anyone was missing out on the riches to be had, it was their fault and not hers. It is true that jobs were to be had in the south-east of England. I would go into the Job Centre on a Monday and have a new job by the end of the week. Jobs, it seemed, fell off trees like apples. The mood in Kent was buoyant and positive. You could see that people were doing well. The company that fitted the new kitchen into my parents' house had an order book that was overflowing, just like the companies that installed double glazing and those that put in new central heating. Builders were building new houses at an alarming rate. Estate agents had never been busier and banks were doling out mortgages and loans like sweets. The overseas package holiday industry was getting stronger and stronger and new cars were popping up on driveways like flowers in springtime.

Eleven years is a long time to be prime minister. Tony Blair's own reign was also a lengthy affair, with him eventually stepping down to hand the reigns to Gordon Brown. Blair knew that he couldn't go on for ever. Thatcher, however, was having none of that. By the time 1990 came around, people were wondering if she ever had any intention of going. She had guided the Conservatives successfully to three general election victories, she had fought off an invading army, she had ground down the miners and she had survived an assassination attempt. It seemed that she was all-powerful. Then came the poll tax.

Any form of tax is unpopular, even to someone rich, and the poll tax was no exception. Known formerly as the rates, which was a monthly charge paid to local councils by householders, the poll tax was conceived to rake in more money from the British people. Instead of one property being charged a fixed rate, the new tax essentially meant that every adult living in a property would be expected to pay every month a fixed sum to their local council. It was a case of out with the old and in with the new. The new tax was deemed unfair on the grounds that whilst millions of people were discriminated against, others seemed to benefit from the change.

The riots that followed the government's insistence that the new tax was to stay turned London into a battle ground, with rioters fighting the police and essentially the government. Thatcher had seen this all before with the miners' strike, but to have raging battles on London's streets were something she hadn't witnessed since the Brixton riots in 1981. And the rioters had no intention of bowing to her demands. Enough was enough. After ten years of Thatcherism the mood in the land was changing.

The Conservatives were now almost twenty points behind Labour in opinion polls, and by the time 1990 crept round it seemed that her own government was starting to tire of Thatcher. The poll tax had been a terrible mistake, but through her arrogance she just couldn't entertain the idea of relinquishing power. The tax stayed and the unrest grew. Her crown was slipping, and by the time the first leadership challenge took place she was already wounded. She survived the first round of voting, but come the second round she knew that she was history.

Her eleven-year reign was over. She who had grabbed Britain by the throat in 1979, and shaken it into shape through her boom and bust policies, was to be replaced by her preferred successor, the uninspiring and drab John Major. What hurt Thatcher most was the way her downfall was orchestrated. Men who had once been loyal to her had turned against her. She just couldn't understand it, for it was her who had made those men what they were. But there is no loyalty in politics. You can be here today and gone tomorrow, as Boris Johnson knows only too well. Thatcher's legacy seems glowing, but peel back the paper and you will see massive cracks. You will see division and you will see an overbearing personality that steamrollered through the land. You will see rich people and poor people, but ultimately you will see a tired nation.

8: The Plant Hire Debacle – 1988.

Thinking back, this has got to be the worst job I ever had. Everything about it felt wrong, with me feeling like a fish out of water. It only lasted a year, and during that time I asked myself every day what the hell was I doing working for such a shower of shit, as my employer turned out to be. It was a wasted year, when I could have stayed at the hoverport and at least enjoyed myself, instead of playing the part of a sales assistant in a plant hire shop.

The interview for the job was held in a cramped office under a staircase. The managing director was all smiles and warm handshakes, but his real character came shining through once I was employed as an assistant manager in one of his company's plant and tool hire shops. It was the pay that wooed me, and the talk of 'opportunities to advance.' £8,000.00 a year was big money to me, and a significant increase on what I had been previously earning. I made all the right sounds at the interview, nodding my head whenever my potential employer spoke about how he had created a leading force in plant and tool hire in Kent. He was in love with himself, and I was just wanting to get on the payroll. I could go as far as I wanted, he told me, with perhaps me managing my own branch a year down the line. It all sounded so wonderful, so when he rang me later in the week to tell me that I had got the job I believed that I was finally moving into the big time.

I knew nothing, and still know as much, about mini excavators, scaffolding, cordless drills and chainsaws. Nuts and bolts are still a mystery to me, as are petrol-powered generators and protective clothing. Cement mixers are another mystery, as are drill bits and orbital sanders. But I wasn't to worry, as during the first week on the job I was looked after by two fitters, who spent their days looking busy in a workshop, repairing the plant and tools that the shop's customers hired and returned, usually broken or missing a few parts. On the first day I turned up in my cheap suit, and one of the lads asked me to 'strip down' a chain saw. I took a spanner and decided to get stuck in. I tried to look enthusiastic, but I just didn't get turned on by grease and oil. And anyway, I was an assistant manager. What the fuck was I doing pretending to be a fitter? But it was all part of the training, and I had no choice in the matter. To be fair, my two colleagues were great guys. They were both bikers, and looked like they were part of the Hells Angels. In their workshop was a space for them to have their tea breaks, and they had adorned the walls with pages ripped out of porn magazines. They worked, like all of us, to earn money, and they made it clear that our boss was as appealing as a turd sandwich.

After my induction into the world of oil changes and air filters, I finally got behind the shop counter. The manager was the managing director's brother, and he seemed quite a decent guy. He was friendly enough. Working with him was another man, in his forties, who seemed to be a shop assistant. It transpired that he had actually worked for the company for a few years, and had wanted to become assistant manager. He had however been usurped by me, an outsider, and it didn't please him. To add insult to injury he was going to help me learn the ropes. It didn't bode well for the future, and there was a bad atmosphere about the place during my time there. I really don't know why they hadn't given the job to him, because he was more capable and knowledgeable than me.

The shop itself was situated in a cul-de-sac, in a quaint

setting just outside of Dover. There was ample space in the street for me to park my new car, which was a sky-blue Austin Montego. Thinking back I really liked that car, but all of these years later it makes me chuckle when I recall that I had so much pride in what was basically a pile of junk. Next to the shop was a hair salon, and next to that was a village post office which also doubled up as a corner shop. The residents didn't like to be bothered by the constant coming and goings of trucks and lorries, that turned their cul-de-sac into a noisy neighbourhood from eight o'clock in the morning, and occasionally a member of the blue-rinse brigade would come into the shop and complain to the manager. I was once accosted by a silly old bastard who prodded me lightly with his umbrella, to complain about the noise, but I just brushed him to one side. That old sod is probably long gone, like the shop in which I found myself working in for the following year.

We sold bottled gas, which came in all sizes. There were small bottles which you could pick up with one finger, and massive bloody things that rural home-owners used to heat their houses with. Those bottles stood almost as high as me, and weighed nearly fifty kilogrammes. And I should know, because during my first week in the shop the manager decided it was me who was going to do the daily gas delivery. This was more training for me, so that I could get a feel of what went on in the shop. So I drove the truck to the gas compound, loaded it up and set off on my travels. It should have only taken me four hours, but because I had trouble lifting those big bottles onto the back of the truck, I spent eight hours on the job. When I returned to the shop, it was closing time, my back was aching and I was freezing cold and filthy. Not to worry, though, because I had completed my mission. I went home and wanted to cry. The next day was more of the same, except when I pulled out of the yard in the truck I miscalculated the sharp turn, and managed to completely   obliterate the side of a customer's car. I received a written warning for that, and was duly confined to the shop for the rest of my brief career.

I'm not a people person, so standing behind a counter being nice to people isn't in my blood. In the week it was mainly builders who came into the shop, to hire the big stuff. They would reel off a list of their requirements and I would try and understand what they were asking for. I was doomed from the beginning and I didn't really want to be there. It was always the same people who came in, making irrelevant conversation and talking utter gibberish. They always wanted special drill bits and abrasive sheets for their orbital sanders. I'd just scratch my head and try and look as though I was in charge, which I was when the manager was absent. Weekends were slightly more relaxed affairs. The shop closed at twelve noon, and in the morning it was more genial and calm. You'd get old biddies coming in for a paint brush or married men looking for a rechargeable drill to buy. I actually became quite good at selling stuff on Saturday mornings, because I was less stressed out. And then Monday morning would come back round, and the misery would start all over again.

My colleagues weren't too bad, apart from the one who I had usurped. He would, however, eventually leave and go and work for another plant hire company. The relief felt when he left gave me a new boost of enthusiasm, as did the arrival of a new manager. Things seemed to be looking up for me, but any renaissance was to be short lived. If the highlight of my time working for the company had been a staff day trip to France, which involved eating steak and chips and getting drunk on cheap wine, the low point came with the appointment of a general manager. From that moment on I was on borrowed time.

He was a right bastard, although on our trip to Calais he had come across as charming and friendly. But he was neither of these things. He had six shops to oversee, and he spent most of his time driving from shop to shop berating the staff for no apparent reason. He carried a mobile telephone which resembled a house brick, and used to bellow into it when insulting some poor sod on the other end of the line. He had his favourites, like all managers, and I wasn't one of them. I would never be a manager with my own company car, that was for sure. I was nothing in that shop, and with the piss-pot of a general manager that's how it was going to stay. Oh, yes, he liked a drink. There was a pub a short walk from the shop, and whenever he came by to visit us, he would time his visit to coincide with the opening of the pub at lunchtime. And off he'd go for a few pints, before returning two hours later tanked up. You could smell the beer a mile away, and he would wish us a cheery goodbye before driving off.

I got to like my new manager, but his career with the company was destined to be as short-lived and unspectacular as my own. The general manager didn't like him from day one, as he probably felt threatened by someone who had a better knowledge of the industry than himself. So here we were hiring out cement mixers and selling cordless drills, whilst behind the scenes a power struggle was unfolding. It was the sort of stuff that high-flying executives in the city of London are familiar with, in their cut-throat world in which they operate. But this was just a tale of egos playing out a Shakespearian tragedy in a leafy cul-de-sac, where the curtain-twitching residents would have laughed out loud if they had known about what was going on in their neighbourhood. At times it was farcical, and then it was ridiculous. But that vile little turd with his brick-sized telephone and penchant for a few pints at lunchtime wouldn't let the new man get the better of him. One of them had to go, and the loser was my only ally in the shop. He just gave up, left and got himself a job with another company.

The arrival of yet another new manager only compounded my misery, for he was a friend of the general manager. He had been shoehorned into the job, and so I started to make concerted efforts to make my own exit as soon as possible. I couldn't have stayed there, because the clouds hanging over me were getting heavier, and I was feeling depressed. This was no way for a young man to be living. I should have been happy at work and happy at home, but instead I was moody and miserable. That bloody was shop was to blame, with its stifling atmosphere and power-crazy personnel. I hadn't signed up for the kind of shit I was taking, but that's what I was enduring. And this is when I learnt a very important lesson in life, that being that you should never believe what people tell you, even if they're your friends.

When Bob, the previous manager, had been gone for a few months he invited me to a barbecue at his house. We had kept in touch and had become friends, and so I thought that a chance to catch up with him would do me the world of good. The barbecue was a mediocre affair, with some very boring people having been invited. But it was good to see Bob, and as the evening went on he told me that he had found another job in the plant hire industry, and was general manager for one of my employer's competitors. He had a decent company car and a good salary, and seemed to have landed on his feet. And then he asked me if I wanted to go and work for him, in the capacity of assistant manager in one of his company's branches. Well, I didn't have to think twice, and was already playing out in my mind the scene in which I resigned from my current job, and told the general manager where to stick his oversized telephone. I had found a way out, thanks to Bob, and it all sounded too good to be true. And it was.

The following Monday I resigned. I offered to work my notice out, but when the general manager knew I was going to work for a rival company, and had effectively been poached by Bob, he went into a foul-mouthed rage. He asked me to leave there and then, which didn't particularly bother me. And so I was gone from that shop in the quiet cul-de-sac, where I had never felt welcomed or loved from the very first day of my career with the company. It was early afternoon, and I headed to the local pub to have a couple of pints, just glad that the horror show was behind me. That odious bastard of a general manager had caused so much ill feeling through the company, and he seemed to enjoy wreaking havoc. But now, all of that was behind me.

My new job didn't get off to a flying start. The shop where I worked was a terrible place, and furthermore I was expected to work every Saturday, from nine o'clock in the morning to five o'clock in the evening. The owner was a millionaire property developer and he was omnipresent. Bob was general manager, but only in name. Our paranoid and control-loving paymaster was everywhere and anywhere, and as with a great majority of wealthy, self-made men, he had a phobia of losing his money and felt that his employees were out to fleece him. I was paid every week, by cheque, which seemed a very 1970's way of doing things. The shop itself was a drab, poorly-lit affair, managed by a fat man with greasy hair. Mike was a dull and boring man, and was probably a virgin. He knew the price of everything in the shop, and had a rather sycophantic way of dealing with the customers. He never let me have any interaction with the customers, and most of my time was spent dusting the shelves or sweeping the yard.

A new wave of depression washed over me, and my situation was made worse when Bob was sacked for no apparent reason. He had wanted to change the way things were done in the company, but the owner wasn't having any of it. His old tried and tested ways of doing things were the only way to do things. He wasn't into radical change. Poor old Bob. Out of another job in the space of a few months, and without a car when he was asked to leave behind his Nissan Bluebird. I hung around for a few moths, but the misery running through me was dragging me down and wearing me out. I had only been in the job for eight months when the owner asked to see me in his office. He was sat behind his desk when he saw me, with a massive picture of the Rocky Mountains hanging on the wall behind him. There were a few porcelain clowns scattered throughout his office, as his sole passion was collecting anything and everything to do with them. I was probably one of his clowns, albeit a real one.

I wasn't surprised when he gave me the sack. If anything, I was relieved. He told me to go there and then. I just walked past fat Mike and probably called him something unpleasant. And there I was, as free as a bird. I took Bob off of my Christmas card list, and from that day on I promised myself that I would never be persuaded or influenced by friends. I drove home in my Austin Montego, and after a cup of tea I walked to the unemployment office so I could sign on the dole. That day was a bad day, but on reflection it was nothing to get upset about. It was a couple of kicks in the balls in the space of a year, but this was a time when getting a job was as easy as going out to buy a newspaper.

It was summertime, so I sat around at home for a few months living off the state. The fortnightly dole money was a pittance, but it was enough to buy me a few pints down the pub. And then, when I got bored, I rang the major to see if he had a job for me down the hoverport. He welcomed me back with open arms, and so for the next few months I was back working all hours, for a few hundred pounds. And I felt great, because I felt wanted. I got my head into shape and the black clouds that had been hanging over me were gone. That office wasn't only a place of work, but it was more of a positive, happy place from my past. And when a few months later I got myself a new job, I knew that I would never return there. This time the leaving was for good. But even today, many decades later, I still think about my return to that office, the major and that job. The hoverport is long gone, which is a shame. The shop in the cul-de-sac, where I tried to make a name for myself in the plant hire world is also gone, like all of the other shops owned by my previous employer. His company went bust, which is a shame for the good people who worked for him, but not for those who deserved everything they got.

9: Good Times, Bad Times.

Some good did come out of those turbulent times – or at least I thought so. For a start there was my Austin Montego, which I considered to be classy and eye-catching. I paid £5,000.00 for the car, after immediately falling in love with it. To think that I would be bowled over by such a thing seems totally ridiculous today. It was a British Leyland creation, and to be honest it was crap. To start with it did its job, but after a while niggling mechanical problems started to surface. During its time with me the car was stolen from a car park in Canterbury. It was abandoned by the thieves and found by the police. The thieves were never found, and I was reunited with the vehicle. If they had written off the car I would have at least got paid out by my insurance company. But no such luck there. The battery went flat in the car park at Gatwick Airport. Imagine my joy on discovering that the bloody wouldn't start after a week's holiday in the sun. And finally there was the oil warning light that failed miserably. Those old Leyland creations guzzled oil like there was no tomorrow, as I discovered when the engine seized up in the middle of a busy road. The whole thing had to be replaced, at an enormous expense. In the end I finally got rid of the car and returned to using public transport.

I had a few overseas holidays during the eighties, including a two-week trip to the Dominican Republic. It was the first time I had taken a long-haul flight. The holiday itself went without incident, and those two weeks did me the world of good. A few weeks after my return I would find myself being unemployed, after my ill-fated foray into the world of plant hire. That holiday had burnt up all of my cash, which meant that my financial situation was desperate. And being financially stretched would be nothing new to me, as my inability to control my spending would give me a real headache over the coming years. I'd borrow money from my bank, and when they wouldn't authorise another loan I turned to financing my lifestyle by using credit cards. Eventually I would be going to work just to pay my debts.

Our humble council house was transformed when my parents bought it from the local council, taking advantage of Thatcher's right-to-buy scheme. The old central heating system was ripped out and shiny new radiators were installed. Double glazing was fitted and a new kitchen was put in. The kitchen was one of those eighties creations that looked like something you'd find in a farmhouse. And all of this was paid for with borrowed money, that came in the form of an endowment mortgage. Years later those endowment mortgages were receiving bad press, after having been incorrectly sold to customers, who were promised large returns on their investments. An endowment policy would usually, at maturity, have raised enough money to pay off an accompanying mortgage. However, this wasn't the case, leading to thousands of customers being compensated for being basically ripped off by their banks. My parents would later get compensation from their mortgage provider, for being sold a basically useless policy. And so the days of the endowment mortgage were over.

Dad's wages weren't going up in line with inflation, and so the ability to repay their loans, put food on the table and pay the household bills was becoming difficult for my parents. Mum worked part time at Marks and Spencer, and her pay wasn't fantastic. I'd give them some money at the end of every month, which was money that I was having difficulty in finding myself. The eighties were being kind to a lot of people, but for others it was a difficult time. When dad died in 2008 he was physically broken by his illness, and under a lot of pressure financially. The loans had piled up, from the eighties, and twenty years later his health had started to suffer. He should never have been given so much money, but back in the eighties the banks and building societies were just interested in lining their own pockets. It was a period of irresponsible lending and profiteering.

Estate agents and pension salesmen were having a field day. When the economy was bouncing along there was money to be made. Yuppies were born in this era, a creation of Thatcher's premiership. They were making millions on the stock market, and living the high life. They would have been more than disappointed when everything came crashing down around them, in the very same decade when they saw the light of day. They were literally here today and gone tomorrow, with their mobile telephones and expensive champagne. Greed was a product of the decade, when the city boys wanted more than was reasonable. And all of a sudden those jobs that grew on trees were getting difficult to come by. The north of England was ravaged by unemployment, and the south was starting to suffer.

Yet still people voted for Thatcher and her government. She was in power right throughout the eighties, seemingly indestructible. When she seemed down and out she would bounce right back. Her victory over the Argentinian invaders in the Falkland Isles gave her some breathing space. Arthur Scargill took her to the wire, but she ground the miners down until they eventually returned to work. She survived an assassination attempt at the hands of the I.R.A. Even they couldn't work out how she had not been killed when they exploded a massive bomb in the Grand Hotel, in Brighton. She did a lot of good, but she did more harm. But in the eighties people were blind to what was really happening. It's only years later that the cracks she papered over have come to light.

I never voted in any elections in Britain. The reasons to do so were numerous, and the Conservatives were so all-powerful that the opposition were never going to get elected. Today they have been in power for over a decade, and Britain is in a terrible mess. But still people put faith in the government. Still the people fall for the same old lies and deceit. The people prefer to stick with who they know, rather than take a chance on someone new. Tony Blair did successfully buck the trend in 1997, when his New Labour party swept to victory, with Blair serving as prime minister for the following ten years, before handing over the reigns of power to Gordon Brown. Unfortunately for him, Brown's tenure coincided with the global financial meltdown, which meant his premiership would be remembered for all of the wrong reasons. With the British economy in tatters, he would be ousted at the following election, to be replaced by David Cameron and his Conservative government.

But even in those turbulent and unsettled times, some things would ride out the storm. I remember on Friday and Saturday nights that Deal's pubs would be bursting at the seams. Pints of lager were consumed at an alarming rate, and the ambiance in those pubs was electric. The music was quality, people were allowed to smoke inside and there was a general feeling of good times in the air. Deal seafront was lined with pubs that were doing a roaring trade. You couldn't get inside some of them because it felt like the world and its mother was standing at the bar. And if there were occasional fights after hours, no-one thought about stabbing people to settle an argument, as is the case today. Four decades later and Friday and Saturday nights are a lot calmer. Thousands of pubs have gone, and peoples' habits have changed. The price of a pint of lager has become too much for many people, and now the new generation of drinkers are staying indoors and drinking their supermarket alcohol. The Covid-19 disaster pushed a lot of pubs towards the abyss, but to be fair many of them were struggling before.

The High Street is another aspect of our lives that has taken a turn for the worse. Saturdays would sometimes be about going into town, to browse in the local shops and then pop into a pub for a pint or two. Deal, in the eighties, boasted a Marks and Spencer and a Woolworths. For a quaint and charming seaside town, it certainly had a great High Street. The big out-of-town supermarkets were yet to change our shopping habits, so for food shopping Deal's main shop was a grubby-looking and outdated Tesco. The shop closed when Tesco built a massive store on an industrial park in Dover. Still there today, it opens virtually twenty-four hours a day, seven days a week. Needless to say it sells everything from avocados to flat-screen televisions. When they started selling baguettes in the Deal store, it seemed like a revolution had happened. The advent of the internet and online shopping smashed through the High Street and made buying clothes, tins of beans and electrical items a whole lot easier and more convenient. I mean, who likes going shopping when it's raining and freezing cold? Queuing to pay is a thing of the past. Now the supermarket chains will pack your bags for you and deliver your groceries to your door. Whatever you may think, for a lot of people this service is a godsend. The downside is that the big retail names have suffered. There's not as many people going into their stores today. Woolworths is long gone and Marks and Spencer, once the glittering jewel in any High Street, is on its knees. Deal High Street is dead on its feet. Both of the big names have gone for good. When once it was full of life, Deal's High Street is now moribund.

In the eighties getting a job was all about going to the Job Centre or replying to an advert in a newspaper. Four decades later the internet has changed all that. Saturday mornings would have meant standing in a queue at the bank, to pay in a cheque or to ask for an overdraft. My bank was in an impressive-looking building, and the queues never moved very fast. My request for an overdraft was always refused, because back then I was a bad risk. Today, through online banking, you can get a credit card and a loan in a matter of minutes. Banks need to grow to survive, so borrowing money has certainly become a lot easier.

The thing that really strikes me is how people today seem to run around at a hundred miles an hour. People today never seem to sit still and take five minutes to relax. When I was growing up Sundays were all about sitting around the dining table and enjoying a roast lunch. The radio would be on and there would be a handful of newspapers to browse through. Sometimes we'd go for a walk after lunch, to see what was happening in the world. There were no shops open and fast food wasn't really part of Sunday lunch. Now those big out-of-town stores are open on Sundays, and McDonald's is where you'll find a lot of families tucking into their Happy Meals, as they browse through their text messages and social media accounts.

10: A New Start – 1990.

The idea of someone borrowing a hundred pounds, and repaying the loan every week from the comfort of their own home seemed a strange concept to me. I mean, who the hell would borrow such a small sum of money, and repay four pounds every week to a doorstep collector? And then again, who would order a Christmas hamper in June, pay three pounds a week for it, before having their hamper delivered in time for Christmas? But this was how Provident Personal Credit made their money, and it was with the Provi', as it was more commonly known amongst its employees and customers, that I would spend the next two years of my working life.

I answered the advert that appeared in one of those free newspapers that seemed to be shoved through the letterbox on a regular basis. The last few pages were for situations vacant, and scanning the pages I saw that a nationwide finance company were looking for a section manager for their branch in Dover. There wasn't much information in the advert, but nonetheless I telephoned the number given and asked for an application form to be sent to me. Two days later I received the form, and after filling it in I sent it back to the branch manager, not overly optimistic about my chances of being called for an interview. After all, my C.V. was hardly bulging with quality and expertise, with it being more of a tale of woe and failings. The plant hire episode stuck out like a sore thumb, and my two stints at the hoverport were not really going to have potential employers chasing after me.

The Montego was off the road when the call came. Another oil leak had consigned it to my uncle's garage for reparations. The car that only a few years earlier had been my pride and joy had now turned into a bloody nightmare. If it wasn't pissing out oil or water, the bloody thing didn't want to start on cold mornings. Then there was the rust that was slowly starting to take hold of the sky-blue paintwork. The jokes that do the rounds on social media about British Leyland and the crap cars that were made by Britain's number one car manufacturer are all true. The company took a lot of stick back in the seventies and eighties, most of which now appears to be warranted. When the company unleashed the Mini Metro onto the public in the eighties, it did so hoping to transform it fortunes. But like all of its ancestors that came off the British Leyland production lines, the latest creation would be destined for the same negative treatment.

I had bought a new suit from Burton's a few months earlier, and it was a marked improvement on the one I had been using over the previous few years. My latest acquisition was smart and fitted well, unlike the shiny number I had bought in Foster Menswear after I had left school. I had also bought a new pair of black shoes, which squeezed my toes together after wearing them for just a few minutes. But the pain that came from having my feet compacted by size-nine footwear would be a small price to pay, if at the end of the day I had got myself a new job. And so I was full of confidence when I took the short train ride from Deal to Dover, making sure that I didn't sit on chewing gum or scuff my shoes along the way.

The office, which is now long gone, was situated above a gents outfitters. A side door lead to a steep flight of stairs, which took me for the first time to what would eventually be my workplace for the following two years. On the first floor there were several offices, leading off from a poorly-lit corridor, at the end of which was a wooden chair. After announcing my visit to one of the girls in the reception office, I was asked to take a seat. And there I waited for a few moments, looking around me and breathing in the nicotine-laced air that seemed to hang over the place. The walls were a deep orange colour, and the whole place looked like it had been going downhill since the previous decade.

A little fellow, with a thick Irish accent and orange fingers, introduced himself to me. He was the branch manager. He was smoking a cigarette when he shook my hand. I followed him into his office, where the stench of cigarette smoke was omnipresent. I took a seat and he offered me a cigarette. Was it a test, or was it a show of kindness? Was it the done thing to accept a cigarette from a man who could be my future manager? I accepted his offer, because a free cigarette should never be refused. My interviewer then started to reel off a series of questions, which I responded to with ease. He was a company man, who knew everything there was to know about the Provi'. It seemed he was part of the furniture, which, in his office, seemed outdated and in need of replacement. The interview lasted an hour, in which time a vast number of cigarettes were smoked. He seemed impressed by me. We stood up at the end of the interview and shook hands. It was then that I noticed his bright red face. I imagined that he enjoyed a drink, and I was right. Booze and cigarettes, after all, usually went hand in hand. He thanked me for taking the time to see him, and he announced that he would be in touch, if I was to be called back for a second interview.

I didn't like that feeling of not knowing what was going to happen next, but I had to wait and see if the call came. After changing out of my suit, I went round to my uncle's garage to collect my car. It was another bill to pay, and that bloody car was burning up my money. I was hardly the richest man in town, but if was successful in getting the job, I needed a car. I didn't have enough money to buy a better model, and I was still paying the loan back to the bank for the Montego. So until my luck changed, and I was in a position to buy a better car, I had to make do with what I had. Over the next three years my pride and joy would be in and out of the garage on a regular basis. Mechanically it was a total nightmare, and the more it cost me in repairs the more I ended up hating it. Its engine would eventually seize up on the road between Deal and Dover, when it had to be recovered by a breakdown vehicle. I paid over a thousand pounds to replace the engine, which turned out to be another waste of money. I eventually sold the vehicle for a few hundred pounds, after it failed its M.O.T. I used the money to go on a cheap holiday, with me still owing the bank a few thousand pounds on the loan I had originally taken out for the car.

A week later I was invited back for a second interview. This time the branch manager was accompanied by a stocky guy, who wore sunglasses. He was the area manager. He shook my hand and nearly crushed my fingers, such was the pressure he applied on them. People who wear sunglasses indoors are are one of the many things I dislike. Outside, in summer, I can understand, but I find it disconcerting that people feel the need to wear them inside. I like to see peoples eyes when I speak to someone, because I can gauge if they're being sincere. Tea was served in a chipped mug, but there were no cigarettes this time. The branch manager was less chatty in the company of his superior. The air was more formal and less relaxed than the first time. The area manager seemed impressed by what I had to say. I just told him that I was keen to build a career, and could adapt to most situations. This is a line I always used when being interviewed for a job, and it seemed to be what potential employers wanted to hear. He swallowed the bullshit and announced that I had got the job. I was to be a section manager at the Dover branch of Provident Personal Credit. We discussed my salary, which would be the most I would earn since leaving school. I would also be required to attend a four-week training course, in the company's head office in Bradford. The company would pay for accommodation for me in a nearby hotel, in Bingley. It all sounded like great fun, and when I left the office I breathed a huge sigh of relief. I had finally got a job that had real prospects, working for a company that invested in its staff. And furthermore, I was a section manager. That wasn't bad, I thought, for someone with only two 'O' Levels.

Much beer was consumed that evening, to celebrate the page being turned in my professional life. The disaster that had been my foray into the world of plant hire was finally forgotten. Now I was going in the right direction. My new job sounded like it wouldn't be too difficult, and I was convinced that if I did well I would soon be looking to become a branch manager. And that was the dream that had been sold to me. That was what the area manager wanted. He wanted motivated young men and women to do well, because his success depended on it.

But before any of that could happen, there was the matter of the four-week training course, in Bingley. I had never been so far north before, so my trip to West Yorkshire was going to be an experience for me. I carefully hung my only suit in the back of my car, and loaded a bag with clean underwear and shirts. I prayed to the Almighty one for his assistance in making sure my car made it to its intended destination, without breaking down. It was going to be the first long haul for the Montego, and I wasn't sure how it would handle the journey. But I needn't have worried, because after gently heading up the M1 motorway on the following Sunday afternoon, I made it to Bingley without any problems. It seemed like that perhaps everything was slotting into place.

11: Boredom & Beer – 1990.

Training courses, as I discovered, are tedious affairs. And those ran by Provident, in their Bradford head office, were no different. The day would always start well, with a decent English breakfast in the hotel restaurant. Then it would be off across town, to one of West Yorkshire's old industrial centres, that by now was looking very frayed around its edges. To be fair, the people are a friendly lot. They're quite cheerful and have an accent that generates some warmth and kindness, as opposed to people from my neck of the woods, who don't have an accent and appear, at times, to be cold and unloving, whenever they speak with their flat and lifeless tones.

I think, if I remember rightly, that there were six of us being trained. I got on straight away with a couple of the guys with me, who, like me, showed a lack of enthusiasm from the very start of our time on the course. The training officers did their best to liven up proceedings, but how can you make what is basically a debt collector's job sound exciting? Yes, although we were section managers, we soon understood that our main role in life was to go out knocking on doors and shaking up late payers. That didn't particularly bother me, but what did irritate me was the constant regurgitating of information that we were being subjected to. Those four weeks could have been squeezed into two, if those bloody people who had devised the training programme had chopped out a lot of the useless stuff.

At lunchtime we were let out of our classroom to eat a buffet, that was freshly prepared every day by the catering department. Provident's head office was one of those sprawling buildings that was a workplace for hundreds of employees, working on different floors. It was imposing, neat and tidy. On our first day we had a guided tour of the place, and it was only then that I got an idea of just how big my new employer actually was. What had started life as a simple money-lending operation was now a huge concern, with branches all over the country. Its origins were in Bradford, but the company had grown to be a nationwide entity. But the offices were usually well hidden, occupying spaces above existing shops. And, like the Dover office, they all seemed to be in a sorry state of repair, in need of at least a lick of paint. But Provident wasn't a bank, with fancy High Street branches to serve its customers. It was for people who didn't have bank accounts, and whose loans were paid back every week on their doorsteps. The driving force behind Provident were the thousands of collection agents who did their rounds at the end of every week, collecting from their customers. These agents were paid a commission on the money they collected, so it was in their interest to get as many of the repayments that were due. A section manager's job was, as we soon learnt, was to accompany those agents from time to time, to help get money out of the bad payers.

Once the afternoon training session was over it was time to go back to our hotel. Our evening meals were paid for, but not our bar bills. I usually liked to drink four pints of Guinness before dinner, and I discovered that the hotel bar wasn't cheap. Of course, we could have gone to a nearby pub, but the nearest one was a drive away. And, anyway, we were getting to like the hotel, which was similar to the Crossroads Motel. Sometimes we had homework to do, but once the booze started to kick in our evening exercises would usually be completed at the breakfast table. Evenings were for drinking, eating and drinking, and that's all. Once or twice we were reprimanded by our training officers for being too rowdy in the bar.

The hotel had made a complaint to our employer. We had our knuckles rapped and it was soon forgotten.

At the end of the four-week period, with our training over, we were invited to dinner with the company's managing director. He was a decent guy, who had been with the company for years. Having risen through the ranks, he now held the top job. The dinner was a fairly subdued affair, and my intake of Guinness had been curtailed just for once. I didn't want to make a fool of myself in the presence of the top man. Once the evening was over, the managing director shook our hands and wished us well. Now the hard work was to begin. But before all of that, it was back to the bar for a few last pints of Guinness, together with a final evening of friendly banter. From then on we would all be going our separate ways. I would be going to the Dover office, where a host of challenges were awaiting me.

12: A Shit Job, But Someone's Got To Do It – 1990.

I came crashing down to earth with a bump. Friday nights had usually been about staying in to watch television, or venturing into town to enjoy a few pints in my favourite pub. But all of that was over. Friday nights now had me dressed in my suit, driving through council estates in search of my non-paying customers. Thursday nights were also dedicated to debt collecting, trying to squeeze some cash out of someone, before the weekend came, when any spare money the non-payers had would usually be spent on fags and booze. In the daytime I would spend a few hours in my office, preparing my rounds for the evening, like a doctor would prepare his list of house-calls. It was pointless going debt collecting in the daytime, especially in summer, because the non-paying fraternity would be at the beach, or just getting hammered in a pub. And so the best time to catch the little bastards was at night, when they were eating their dinner and looking forward to watching Coronation Street.

To say that you have to be motivated to be a debt collector is an understatement. In the warm months, when the days are long and the sun is permanently shining, trudging along pavements, avoiding the dog shit and empty beer cans, is just about manageable. Up and down the garden paths I would go, ringing the doorbell and waiting for the door to open. On the rougher estates vicious dogs would bark from behind the door. The curtains would twitch, and when the customers saw that I wasn't going anywhere, they'd finally open the door. Some of the dogs leapt up at me, and others just sniffed my suit. And then I'd politely ask for some money, because the customer was behind with their repayments. Many told me to come back the following week, and others would reach into their pockets and pull out a fat bundle of grubby banknotes. They probably had more money on them than I earned in a month. To some customers, not repaying their loan on time was all a bit of fun. It must have made them laugh to see me coming up their garden paths every Friday night, when they knew that I would have preferred to be in the pub. Once or twice I would be invited inside the house, to be offered a cold beer whilst the customer tried to find some money to give me. Then there would be conversation, because sometimes some of the customers were old and lonely. But never once was I threatened with physical violence, because I always showed respect and understanding. I was propositioned once or twice by single mothers, and one perennial non-payer even cooked me dinner.

However, in winter, in the rain and cold, the job took on another less glamorous aspect. I found that peoples' attitudes changed in those dark, depressing months. One of my areas was Aylesham, a village between Canterbury and Dover, which was once a thriving mining community. A large number of men worked in the surrounding mines, and the village, like many others in the region, was prosperous and lively. Those men had money in their pockets to pay for their houses, put food on the table, go on holiday and go to the local club at the end of the every week. By the time I had started my job, Aylesham was very different. The mines were gone and those once proud miners were now unemployed. Streets and streets of households had been affected by Margaret Thatcher's obsession to put an end to the mining industry. The pits were gone and the money had long gone, too. And all of those households had taken out loans with my employer, and none of the loans were now being repaid. It was a hopeless task going from door to door, in the winter months, knowing that there was no money to be had. And those customers weren't faking their financial situation, they really were suffering hardship. The houses were in a poor state of repair and the front gardens were overgrown. Wild dogs barked in the street and rubbish blew around in the wind. The club which the miners had once frequented every Friday night was boarded up, as was the local convenience store. The cars parked in the roads were untaxed, and an air of misery hung over the place. By the time I had left my job, most of those loans had been written off and consigned to history.

Some nights I would go out on my rounds and return a few hours later without having collected a penny from my customers. Winter meant Christmas, and if they couldn't afford to buy presents for their kids, they couldn't afford to repay their loans. It was a soul-destroying job, which gladly did have a few bright moments. John, one of our agents covering part of Folkestone, wasn't really giving his round full commitment. He lacked motivation, so I decided to spend a few Thursday and Friday nights with him, to see if I could make him a better agent. His round was spread out, and he seemed to be doing a lot of miles for very little return. I could see why he was losing interest in the job. John lived near a flat-roofed pub, which, despite the reputation such pubs have, was a friendly place to have a drink. In the end we would go out on his round for a few hours, and invariably give up. We'd then go to the pub and spend the rest of the evening drinking. And that's how my career at Provident would peter out.

When we weren't collecting debts, section managers spent two days a month drawing up lists of good customers – yes, there were a few – to sell household items and jewellery to. The company had a sales division, which was basically traders driving around in vans, selling their wares to existing customers. Ringwould, just outside of Deal, was a popular target area for the traders. The customers weren't the best on my patch, but they certainly weren't the worst. I'd meet the van at the beginning of the afternoon, and the salesmen would start knocking on doors. Eventually a stream of gullible punters would arrive at the van, to see what was being sold. Single mothers would buy packs of poor-quality tea towels, bath towels, cutlery, china plates and cups and whatever other crap was in the van. They'd pay a first payment of fifty pence and then pay a few pounds every week until they had paid for their purchases. It was actually embarrassing to see people paying over the odds for utter tat, but it was all profit for my employer. The salesmen had no scruples whatsoever, and just wanted to offload all of their merchandise as quickly as possible.

The jewellery salesman, however, was in a different class. Mike is one of the drabbest individuals I've ever had the misfortune to work with. He'd visit our office once a month, so that I could supply him with a list of customers who had an excellent credit record, and who could perhaps be persuaded to buy some jewellery from him. We'd then spend the day driving round to the see the customers, hoping to offload some overpriced rings, necklaces and bracelets. The best punters to sell to were those who had a proven record of being able to repay their previous loans on time. Once he had got his foot in the door, Mike never liked to leave without making a sale. The merchandise, which was basically nine-carat gold crap, was kept in a bulky display case, which resembled an overgrown brief case. The case was handcuffed to his wrist whenever he was walking along the street with it, because some of his colleagues had actually been attacked and assaulted by desperate criminals. If they had only known what was in the case, they may have thought twice about trying to have it away.

To be fair, days out with boring Mike were an opportunity to escape from the usual days out debt collecting and getting drenched in torrential downpours. The customers were more refined, and we were always offered a cup of tea or a glass of something stronger. His sales patter was embarrassing, to say the least, but he knew how to make women want to buy his wares. And then, once they were on side, it was only a matter of time before they bought something. The jewellery he flogged was overpriced rubbish, but there were always gullible customers willing to buy something from him. Needless to say, Christmastime was his busiest and most profitable period, and he had no qualms in offloading his jewellery to the customers, knowing that they were paying well over the odds for it. And once the sale was complete, we'd be on our way, leaving the customer happy and leaving our employer satisfied.

My team of collection agents were all women, and they had all worked for the company for years. Most of them had become long in the tooth, and none of them like change. I would accompany a different agent once a week, on their round, to get a feel for our customers. I could see that there was a special bond between some of the customers and the agent, and at times I felt that my presence wasn't really appreciated. The old biddies were set in their ways, and only handed over their money to their personal agent. I was once out on my rounds and tried to collect off a few of them, but they weren't having any of it. They didn't care if I was a section manager – they weren't going to hand over their money to me. And it was this feeling of apathy towards me that finally left me thinking that my career wasn't probably the right one for me.

Eventually I just couldn't be bothered to go out at night on my rounds. What was the point? It was only to see the same old people, who in turn would give me the same old bullshit. Occasionally, if an agent was ill, I would have to cover for them. God only knows how many hours I spent weaving my way through council estates, knocking on doors, collecting a few pounds here and there. A lot of people refused to pay me. They would prefer to wait to pay their agent. I explained that the agent was sick, but it was like pissing in the wind. I'd eventually give up and find a nearby pub to have a few pints in. I would, on returning to the office, be berated by my manager, who wanted to know why I hadn't called on half of the customers. The agent would then give me a blasting, because I had been rude to their most valued customers. It really was a no-win situation in which I found myself.

Occasionally I would have to attend training courses, which were to refresh tired and jaded section managers. Listening to a boring sod rabbiting on about being positive was all I needed. The training officers really had no grasp of the difficulties of the job, believing that their text-book fairy tales related to real life. Nick was one of those boring trainers, who liked to tell unfunny jokes. It turned out he was a failed branch manager, who had saved his own skin in the nick of time by retraining to be a training officer. He looked through rose-tinted spectacles, and couldn't understand why his trainees had become disillusioned, tired and unmotivated. He had an answer for everything, and was the type of guy who I would have liked to have punched in the mouth, after a few pints of strong lager.

And then it would be back to Dover, and back to the soul-destroying realities of the job. By now my motivation was rock bottom, and I really couldn't be bothered to go out and do what I was being paid to do. I started to sympathise with my worst customers, whenever any of them would invite me into their homes for a drink.

My agents were becoming a massive pain in the arse, with their constant moaning, groaning and whining. One of them told me that she was having a hard time trying to to earn a decent living. I just replied that if she wasn't happy then she could fuck off. She looked at me and said that she didn't like the way I had spoken to her. I repeated my last statement, and off she went to complain to the manager.

With the end not far away, the constant misery was briefly interrupted by our Christmas party. All managers, section managers and receptionists were invited to London, to enjoy a party aboard a tourist boat that had been hired for the day. Gently drifting along the river Thames, eating canapés and drinking lager, wasn't really my idea of having fun. To make matters worse, our employer hadn't booked us hotel rooms for the night, which meant we had to drive back to Dover in the evening. I don't know why, but I had been nominated as the driver, using my own car to drive my colleagues back to base. I was a picture of total stone-cold sober misery, as we sped back towards the Kent coast in my Austin Montego, with my four colleagues high on booze. The inside of the car smelt like a brewery. Once I had dropped them off at the office, I just headed to the nearest pub for a few well-deserved pints of lager.

When the area manager, who had interviewed me for the job, was sacked for fiddling his expenses, his replacement made his presence felt almost immediately. He was a tough-talking northerner, who had gradually climbed his way up the corporate career ladder. The Dover branch had become a total shambles, and he was dissatisfied with the performance of the manager and the two section managers. One day he joined me on my rounds. I drove us to Aylesham, in the pouring rain. At first, no-one bothered to open their door to us, until a perennial non-payer greeted us with a friendly smile. On the doorstep, in the pissing rain, I managed to negotiate a payment of fifty pence. The customer was actually hundreds of pounds in arrears. Once back in the car the new area manager shook his head in disbelief. Fifty pence, apparently, wasn't enough. What the fuck did he expect? No-one worked in Aylesham. Fifty pence was a lot of money in that part of the world.

The new area manager would be on our backs over the coming months. The other section manager left, tired of being permanently harassed. I kept my head low, and was by now looking for my own escape route out of the madhouse. Our performance was going from bad to worse. Sales were rock bottom and the number of non-payers was exploding. In the end I couldn't be bothered to go out on my rounds. I'd call into the office for a few hours in the morning, and then return home, to watch television and have a couple of pints in my local pub. My briefcase was bulging with reports and call-lists. I'd occasionally drive over to Folkestone, to meet up with John, for a few pints and a chat. And this glorious period of idleness would be enjoyed, until I finally left the company to move on to pastures new.

13: Reflections – 1992.

The eighties were well and truly over. Margaret Thatcher was gone, having been brought down by her own people. With her demise in 1990, the feel-good days evaporated as quickly as they had been born. She had overseen Britain's most prosperous modern-day decade, from the start to the end, and through her government's policies her reign had improved the fortunes of many people, just as it had compounded the misery of many more. Her dull-as-ditchwater replacement, John Major, inherited her crown, and all of the problems that came with it. The golden decade was over. A new age was in the making. All of a sudden things were becoming more and more difficult. The country was in a recession from 1990 until early 1993, and so those jobs that had been so easy to find were no longer there. The economy had gone into reverse, and people were now losing their jobs. Under Major's leadership, the Conservatives would win the 1992 general election, but the people would finally tire of them come the next election, in 1997, when Tony Blair's revamped and reborn Labour party swept to power.

It was no longer the time to quit a job on Monday, thinking you'd find a new one of Tuesday. Now, I had to find a new job before I resigned from my current one. And then there were fewer jobs and more people on the job market. The nineties would fuck up a lot of things for a lot of people. The recession was a crippler, throwing peoples' lives into disarray. Money was tight, with mortgages and fancy cars having to be paid for. And when people lost their jobs, they still had to pay off their credit card debts. My last days at work for Provident brought home the misery of the situation. Even our good customers were now struggling, too embarrassed to answer the door to me. Some of them used to repay a fifty pounds a week, without fail, at the same time on the same day of the week. Now they were unemployed, and had joined their non-paying counterparts. They would say that they had been good customers, but now, because times were hard, they needed Provident to show sympathy. They didn't realise that business was business. All loans had to be repaid, irrespective of their previous glowing history and the situation in which they now found themselves. I think I upset a lot of 'good' people during my final days with Provident.

My next job had disaster written all over it, proven by the fact that I only lasted thirty days in the employment of the Prudential, the established and respected insurance company. If there was one job I should never have got, it was this one. How the hell I got through the interview is a miracle. And then, somehow, I sailed through the two-week training course like an old professional. And so I found myself working out of the Folkestone office, with a list of potential customers a mile long. It sounded too easy to be true, when my manager said that everyone wanted to buy a policy from the Prudential. Four weeks later, with those words still ringing in my ears, I decided that not everyone wanted to buy something from me.

My career was so brief that I only got paid twice, and on each occasion the pay was pitiful, to say the least. This was due to the fact that as a salesman I was paid a fixed monthly salary of a few hundred pounds a months, together with any commission due on any financial products I sold. During my time with the Prudential I only sold one insurance policy, the reward for which was a few pounds on top of my regular pay. It soon struck me that to earn big money, I would have needed to sell an unrealistic number of products every month.

Being a door-to-door salesman is probably the hardest job in the world. You need to be motivated and full of confidence, as you trudge those unfriendly streets, knocking on doors, looking to sell vacuum cleaners, encyclopedias and products that will simplify everyday life. Selling insurance is just as difficult, as I discovered in the first week in my new job. When I had worked for the Provident, it was all about collecting debts, which in itself can be hard. But those days now seemed like a walk in the park, as my drive and determination drained from me at an alarming rate.

My manager was a decent enough man, but he was so fucking boring, as most people who work in insurance tend to be. At first he came out with me on a few calls, to try and cajole me and help me hone my skills. But it was never going to be. I think the only policy I sold was to a working-class couple, who probably regretted agreeing to see me. I did however get them to sign on the dotted line, which seemed to impress my manager. I drove home that night and wanted to cry. My financial situation was dire and once again, as so often had been the case in my disaster-filled life, I found myself doing a job that I loathed.

When I resigned my manager tried to persuade me to give it another go. But I was out of there quicker than a flying bullet. Unfortunately I forgot to hand in my Psion electronic organiser and calculator, which was required to work out the benefits of the complex insurance policies for the clients. That bloody thing was of no use to me, but I kept it with a view of selling it in the classified section of a local newspaper. The Prudential sent me a letter, asking for the return of the organiser. I ignored the first letter, which was duly followed by a demand for money to pay for the useless piece of crap. I never responded to that letter, and after a while my former employer just gave up. I tried to sell the organiser, but it turned out that it was totally worthless. It ended its life at the rubbish tip.

And so I was now unemployed, in a time when everyday life was becoming harder and more difficult. I couldn't have entertained the idea of adding my two-month career with the Prudential to my C.V., because any future employer would have been put off by what was essentially a bad track record. So I decided to concoct a false entry, in which I claimed to have been an office manager for an independent insurance broker, in Deal. I made out that I had been employed for a number of years, and had been quite successful. Sadly, my employer burnt down his company's office, was paid out by his own insurance company and had emigrated to Australia. And I was now out of work. If any potential employer believed that pack of lies, God was clearly smiling down on me.

But smiling down on me, he was, for a few weeks later I landed what was to be my last job in Britain, before I would eventually turn my back on my homeland, to sail across the Channel, to set up life in France. But that one-way trip was seven years in the making, and before then I had my new job to be getting on with. And this new job promised so much, because it was with what was, at the time, the biggest commercial and private bank on the planet. It was an American corporate monster which gobbled up everything and anything in its path, to become the world's biggest money machine. And there I was, part of it, in my new role as a customer service adviser. It all sounded quite exciting, and Alan, my new boss, promised me that I could go on to be something important if I got stuck into my new job and proved that I had ambition and desire.

14: The New Boy In The New Job – 1993.

In my new, cheap-looking suit, I listened intensely as Tracy, my new colleague, explained the company's outdated computer system to me. She then looked at me and asked me if I was nervous about starting my new job. I said that I wasn't, even if I was lying. I mean, there seemed so much to take in, and I asked myself if being part of a corporate monster was really for me. Then her telephone rang. I answered it, in the robotic style that the company's operating manual insisted that all calls should be answered. It was someone who wanted to borrow money to buy a new fleet of lorries. I was already lost in the conversation, but I continued to listen to the caller, because how else was I going to learn?

And this was how my first week went. When I wasn't answering the telephone, I was sat in my orange work station filling out proposal forms and twiddling my thumbs. Everything furniture related, in the office, looked like it came out of the 1970s. Orange was everywhere, and quite frankly it looked quite hideous. In the corner of the large open-plan office there was a tall potted plant, next to a couple of orange sofas, which visitors sat on, whilst waiting to see Alan, the Emperor. The atmosphere in the office was subdued and there wasn't a lot of laughter to be heard. Perhaps, I thought, it was forbidden. The other thing that struck me was that in the morning, when the employees arrived, they never smiled and said good morning to their co-workers – an American term which was one of the many I would come across during my seven-year stint in the shit-hole that was my place of work. Alan would sail in at eight o'clock every morning, and seemingly glide across the carpet as if he had magical powers. Now that rude bastard would never say hello or good morning, as he disappeared into his corner office. He was as cold as ice, and he always seemed to have the same semi-painful expression etched onto his lifeless face.

In a few weeks I had got to know my colleagues better. There were a few vulgar dogs, and a receptionist who appeared not to get out much. She was boring, and always complaining about the fact that she was underpaid. She had a dodgy left eye, which seemed to aim away from her face whenever she spoke to someone. Whilst Alan was the top man, his assistant was a rather odious individual, who seemed to have an inferiority complex concerning his small stature. Gareth was the manager, and he took his responsibilities lightly. He was sarcastic and generally unpleasant. The little man had his desk at the back of the office, and us mere mortals had our desks arranged in a single file, with our backs turned towards him. I didn't really have much time for my colleagues, although over time newcomers would arrive and old faces would depart. But Alan and Gareth seemed to be there for the long term, a fact that started to eat away at me from almost my very first day at the company.

Those early days were uneventful, although I sensed that Alan didn't really like me. He was like that, in the way that he could just silently convey the message that I wasn't good enough for him and his little piece of the empire. The fact that I had been born and raised on a council estate probably went against me, because Alan was a terrible snob. Then there were my cheap suits and plastic-looking shoes, and the fact that I didn't speak with a plum in my mouth. Alan was, in fact, to become a terrible thorn in my side, and I often asked myself why he had employed me. He spoke very little to most people, and so I wondered just how the end-of-year Christmas party was going to pan out.

I have never liked Christmas office parties. They are tedious affairs, in which the principal players are usually people who can't control themselves once they've had a few drinks. My first Christmas do took place at an Italian restaurant, and we were only a few to attend the evening, because at that time there weren't many of us working at the office. The number of employees would soon swell, later on, when the office would be forced to launch itself into a massive expansion program. But that was all in the near future, and ignored, as I smiled politely and made small talk with my colleagues.

The food was typical Italian fodder, and Alan tried to dazzle us with his knowledge of fine wines, when he ordered the drinks to accompany our meal. But I could see right through him, and his way of putting us all down a peg or two. The evening dragged on without any incident, because no-one had the balls to liven the proceedings up. Gareth was the only one who got drunk, slurring his words at the end of the evening. His liking of booze would later lead to his downfall, which was an event that brought pleasure to many people.

By the time the year ended I had been with my new employer for seven months. To say I was unimpressed would be an understatement. I was poorly paid and my future prospects seemed bleak. It just didn't seem right to me. I was working with some of the dullest individuals I had ever seen, and my two superiors seemed to have it in for me. And if all of that seemed bad, things were going to get decidedly worse.

15: The Pub – 1994.

From my office window I could see the pub on the opposite side of the road. It stood there like a haven from the stormy weather which appeared to shadow me perennially. Up to then I had resisted the urge to start drinking at lunchtime, thinking that the smell of alcohol on my breath would perhaps diminish my chances of promotion. But when the office was visited by the American managing director of the British part of the global organisation, who completely ignored me, I assumed quite rightly that I wouldn't be ascending the corporate career ladder in the near future. He was an ignorant piece of shit, who spoke with a booming voice. This, however, would be the only time our paths would cross, as he would later be sacked after his superiors felt that new American blood was needed in the U.K. This was a ruthless side of the powers that be which was often shown, when a change of leadership was needed, because you don't get to become number one if you have dead wood working for you. Alan was delighted when his superior returned to the other side of the Atlantic, finding it hard to conceal his dislike of his former boss. His joy, however, would be short lived.

The pub would eventually bleed me financially dry, as every lunchtime I would swiftly down four pints of Guinness followed by a whisky chaser. The landlord was a decent fellow, and he would have my first pint served and on the bar, by the time I arrived just after noon. During that mad hour I would usually shovel twenty or thirty pounds into the fruit machines, hoping to win the jackpot. Occasionally I would win a significant prize, but throughout a month I would always be running at a massive loss. By the time the end of the month came round my bank account was heavily in the red. My financial situation would take an even worse turn a few months later, when I decided to use my credit card to pay for a holiday to Las Vegas. The trip cost me seven hundred pounds, and I blew another two thousand pounds on the roulette tables and slot machines. By the time I boarded the plane to fly back home I was broke. The credit card company started to telephone me at my office, asking when I was going to start paying back the debt. I only managed to pay a few hundred pounds back, before the card was cancelled by the provider. I now had a poor credit rating and was extremely depressed.

I was now technically working for nothing. My bank overdraft swallowed up most of my pay, and my days were spent answering calls from my bank and loan companies. My gambling habit, which I still have, had more or less ruined me. Then, to make matters worse, Alan launched a new offensive against me. He hauled me over the coals, telling me that I was useless and that I had to pull my finger out of my arse. By then, my only allies had gone, and it seemed that the whole world was against me. But I wasn't going anywhere. I had Alan weighed up, and I knew that whilst he was lording it up over his part of the empire, that would all change if new blood, mightier than him, was brought in. He really did think he was untouchable, but his cocky attitude was his Achilles heel. His other problem was Gareth, his trusted branch manager. Unfortunately, for Alan, one of my colleagues had reported Gareth to head office, complaining about his surly attitude and the fact that he was often hungover when he reported for work in the morning. Alan tried his hardest to protect his manager, but the Americans running the show in Britain didn't like what they had heard. And so one day Gareth was there, and the next day he was gone.

This comical sideshow helped me to forget my own woes. Being broke and in a shit job was bad, but Gareth's overdue demise somehow helped me get through this difficult time. He was replaced by another low-life human being, who turned out to be Alan's prodigy. If Gareth's downfall had been his uncontrollable drinking, Mike, his replacement, certainly wouldn't be following in his footsteps. The new manager was a reformed alcoholic, so turning up for work smelling of the previous evening's beer intake was never going to happen. Gareth had also had a grudge against the world, because of his size. His replacement was much taller, but that was the only positive thing going for him. I recall that my new manager had a weak handshake and perfectly manicured nails. He was also devoid of any personality. Still, Alan liked him, because he was his ears and eyes in the outside office.

By now the American contingency was growing in the U.K., and our tiny part of the global monster was about to receive an almighty kick up the backside. We had been plodding along, with a couple of salesmen and a small office staff. We rarely achieved our monthly sales objectives and we never set the world on fire. Alan ran the office as though it was his own company, and he didn't like outside interference. Being totally deluded, and fuelled by his overpowering ego, he didn't see the changes coming. In fact, the day Gareth was sacked was probably the day it all started to go wrong for a lot of people. I could see that the bastard was starting to feel the heat, but he dug his heels in and started talking in Churchillian tones. He really was totally deranged, and because people were afraid to approach him, his attitude worsened over time.

New staff were recruited and most of the new faces brought some harmony to the place. One of the newcomers was an alcoholic, who seemed pleased to have someone to visit the pub with at lunchtime. By then, my alcohol dependence was spiralling out of control, and the arrival of my new workmate only added fuel to the burning problem. It's worth noting that the lunchtime-drinking problem wasn't just confined to us. The pub has always been an important part of British life, and the number of office workers partaking in a lunchtime pint, or two, at our favourite watering hole was impressive. And this was a time when smoking was allowed inside pubs. When the law was passed banning this favourite pastime of millions of drinkers, including myself, was when the pubs and clubs throughout Britain started to suffer. It really was a kick in the teeth, and caused so much damage, both financially and socially. I cannot calculate how much money I have blown, in my life, on alcohol, cigarettes and gambling. I imagine it runs into tens of thousands of pounds, but I've always consoled myself with the fact that we only live once.

But what did all of these changes mean for me? Well, nothing. Alan still had an axe to grind with me, although I was now surer of myself. I wasn't going anywhere, especially as I had acquired a few needed allies. And so that's all it boiled down to: another constant struggle against those people who just had it in for me. It really was a familiar pattern in my working life, and it may have been one that I had brought upon myself. All I wanted was to be left alone and allowed to get on with my job. But there was always someone, somewhere, who seemed to have it in for me. How I had trudged through the past was how I would trudge through the future. I would never run or stride confidently, because there were too many obstacles.

Apart from the pub opposite the office, bringing some much-needed cheer, Canterbury was a dreadful place to work in. Noted for its impressive cathedral, in the summer months it was a bloody nightmare. The pub would be full of tourists, making a nuisance of themselves. Nineties Britain seemed to appeal to oversees travellers, even if the decade wasn't a patch on its predecessor. The High Street was crammed full of busy big-name shops like Woolworths and Marks and Spencer, and those shops were seemingly doing well. Yet this was probably the beginning of the end for a lot of the big players, although back then people would have laughed if you had told them that the big names would soon start to suffer, as the decade dragged on and a new millennium came into view.

And if outside everything was slowly changing, what radical transformations were taking place in my office? Well, for a start, things had grown over the last few months, and what was once a sleepy outpost was now starting to turn into a small yet powerful monster. The place was often overrun with Texans and New-Yorkers, who seemed to want to know everything about anything that was going on inside those four walls. Alan was now under pressure, and he would remain to be so until the situation in which he found himself became too difficult to handle.

16: The American – 1998

The beginning of the end came for all of us in 1998. The previous few years had been a time of evolution, during which period I had been promoted and had been given the right to have a company car. I was, by then, flying high. Of course, my promotion wasn't thanks to Alan, nor the equally unpleasant office manager, but more to do with the interference from an outside source, whose influence was by far the greatest of all of the players in this story.

Jerry was the American whom head office had installed in our own office in late 1997. He spoke with a nasally voice, and moved stealthily through the office, when he wasn't sat behind his desk, observing us and making notes. Before he had arrived, Alan had always remained in his own corner office, with his door often closed. When Jerry arrived on the scene, paranoia filled Alan, and so now he had taken to leaving his office door open. His ears and eyes in the main office, Mike, also appeared to be on edge on a permanent basis, following the arrival of the American interloper. And watching my two tormentors wriggling, squirming and grimacing would be the highlight of the end of my working life in Britain. It was a spectacle that I would have paid to watch, if it had been necessary to do so. It was a spectacle that unfolded over a few months, and still makes me laugh out loud when I think about it today.

Of course, a blind idiot would have seen what Jerry was up to from day one of his unwanted arrival. He glided in and made friends with everyone. He bought me drinks in the pub in exchange for information about the terrible twins. He smoked cigarettes with me, downstairs from the office, as we exchanged further bits of useful intelligence. And all the while this was going on, Alan was slowly losing his power. And if he thought he was still in charge, Jerry made it clear that it was no longer the case. And so now, limping along like a lame dog, Alan had become an extra in a play about what happens to people who think that they're untouchable. He would soon learn that whilst it takes years to climb up the corporate career ladder, you can fall off it and hit the ground in a matter of seconds.

At first the interloper observed, and then he started to harass Alan. There was a blazing row when Alan told the American to get out of HIS office. That was probably his biggest mistake. He forgot that his paymasters were of the American variety. I was swanning around, watching and smiling as Alan's allies departed one after the other. The office was in a terrible mess. Business was poor and all of a sudden things looked bleak and grim. Alan was now turning up at nine or ten o'clock in the morning, looking like a man spending his last few days on Death Row. His trusted lieutenant, the sycophantic Mike, was fairing equally as bad. His authority was all but gone, and when, one day, I told him to shut the fuck up, he just looked at me and shook his head. Before, it would have been a sacking offence, but that was before the Americans had started to pull all of the strings. Those lunchtime visits to the pub were now all about drinking to the demise of the terrible duo.

And then they were gone. The two rabid dogs had been summoned to head office, where they were both disposed of. Mike was never seen again, but Alan made a final appearance a week later to collect his personal effects. Before his arrival I had smashed his favourite coffee mug, by throwing it against the floor. Bizarrely it was one of the items he came to collect. When his secretary gave him the shattered mug, he just half smiled and shook his head. He realised then that whilst he had been liked by so many people, he had been hated by so many more. His arrogance had been the end of him.

Needless to say, after the downfall of the Emperor and his henchman, the mood in the office lightened. Fridays became dress-down days, when suits and ties weren't required to be worn. Instead jeans and t-shirts were the order of the day. Jerry bought us pizzas and paid for drinks in the pub. Everyone toasted the end of the old regime, and in the drunken state of euphoria no-one ever thought about the future. The summer of 1999 seemed to go on forever, with people telephoning the office to get the latest news. When some people rang enquiring after Alan, we just replied that he had gone. In a drunken moment I told one caller that he had been sacked, and we were glad to see the back of him. His old acquaintances disappeared off the scene and the old guard was eventually replaced by squeaky-clean replacements. It was like a cancerous growth had been removed, and a breath of fresh air was blowing through the office. The age of the dinosaur was over.

After the revolution came an anti-climax. Summer became autumn, and with the falling of the leaves came the news that the office was closing. Head office was transferring its operations nearer to London, citing that Canterbury was hardly the capital of finance and banking. The superiors, were of course, absolutely right. Jerry had been brought in to bring the curtains down. He offered me a job in the new set up, in the new office. I spent a week there to get a feel for the place, but realised that it was game over for me. The cost of relocating would be too much for me to consider, and it felt right that after seven years it was time to call it a day.

My last few weeks working for the company were spent sitting in my office, twiddling my thumbs. Those hour-long lunch breaks that I had become used to had now turned into all-afternoon drinking sessions. By three o'clock in the afternoon I was too inebriated to work, so I spent my time sleeping in my office. There was no law and order in the office, with Jerry just doing his best to keep things ticking over until the final day.

My final pay, together with my redundancy pay, hit my bank account a few days earlier than planned. When I realised that I was sitting on a pile of money, I decided that even if I technically had two days to work to the end of my contract, my time at the bank was finished there and then. I went to the pub and got gloriously drunk. When I got home I threw my beer-stained suit into the dustbin, before crashing down for a well-deserved sleep. I was awoken the following morning by Jerry's telephone call. He wanted to know why I wasn't at work. I told him to fuck off, before slamming down the receiver. I kept hold of my company car for a few weeks, using it to go on a driving holiday through France. When the holiday was over, I returned the car to the company car park. It was filthy from its overseas adventure. But delivering it back clean had never been part of the deal. I stuck the keys under one of the wheel arches and visited the pub, for what would be the final time.

17: The End.

And so my working life in Britain was over. From the very beginning, when I had earned a few pounds a week as a Y.T.S. boy at Pfizer, via a string of underpaid jobs, I had somehow gone out on a high. I had done well, in the end, at the bank. I was earning good money when the curtains came down, and a few head-hunters made some serious propositions to me, if I really wanted to carry on in commercial finance. I was tempted, but it just didn't seem right. I had eventually had fun at the bank, and I knew that if I went elsewhere those good old days would never be relived. And what is more, I had already made plans for the future.

The new millennium came in with a whimper. It was meant to bring with it computer systems that were set to fail on the stroke of midnight, together with a host of other problems. In fact 1999 became the year 2000 quite effortlessly. Yesterday's Britain was now part of Yesterday's thousand-year stretch, in which the land had risen and fallen so many times, throughout the course of history. There had been wars and revolutions, plagues and famine. There had been victories and defeats. There had been golden decades and platinum periods. For me, personally, the eighties had been an exciting time, and I had been of an age lucky enough to appreciate those ten years. The nineties were much different, and at the start of the new millennium things were decidedly different, with the internet having a massive impact on all of our lives.

Jobs of the old variety were slowly getting harder to find. The revolution that came with the advent of the internet meant that so many of the old ways of doing things would soon become obsolete. Online shopping would put an axe through the traditional High Street, and online banking would remove the need to have physical branches and paid employees in those branches. But those shops and banks continued to plod along, just like the insurance brokers and travel agents, until they really did run out of steam, and had the carpet pulled out from underneath them.

The British High Street had been in intensive care for some time, before it finally passed away on the 6th January 2009. Its best years were behind it, remembered fondly by those – almost all of us born in or before the nineties – and mourned by generations of Saturday-afternoon shoppers. The official cause of death was cancer, that had eventually spread through its body in the same manner a wildfire advances through a parched forest. There had been an opportunity to prevent the malady from getting out of control, but because we had grown bored of it, and because technology had come on in leaps and bounds, as it gasped for air we simply turned our backs on it, shrugged our shoulders, and said that all good things must come to an end.

Founded on the 5th November 1909, Woolworths was just ten months away from celebrating its centenary when its final store in Britain closed on the 6th January 2009. The failure of this bastion of the British High Street had been impressive as its origins, and its downfall would be the first true sign that the foundations of a British tradition were starting to weaken and crack under the weight of change and transformation. There may well have been fireworks on the day Frank Woolworth opened his first store, in Liverpool, almost a hundred years earlier, but on the day it died there were only dry throats and a lot of questions asked. How could such an icon be there one moment and gone the next? But, and more importantly, if it could happen to Woolworths, who else could it happen to?

The answer to the first question raised is that, quite simply, no organisation, be it a retail giant or a banking monster, is immune to failure and disaster. Vast amounts of money, and time, will help create corporate giants, just as a lack of money, in a short space of time, will eventually destroy them. And your name means nothing when you have debts of £385 million, as Woolworths had at the time of its demise. The answer to the second question is everyone else – with no exceptions!

£385 million is a lot of money to be owing to the banks, when your house of cards finally comes tumbling down. With 807 stores at the time of its death, this means that each of Woolworths shops had an average negative worth of almost £480,000. That's a colossal sum of money, and a sum that had been steadily growing over the previous few years. Woolworths would had needed to shift tonnes of Pick 'n' Mix sweets and K-Tel Party Hits albums to chip away at that mountain of debt, and to have sold millions of plastic Christmas trees, to have had a chance of surviving. But, as we know, those sales just didn't happen, their stores were stripped bare in a massive closing down sale and the lights finally went out for good on a miserable winter's day. Twenty-seven thousand people lost their jobs as a result of the disaster, and huge gaps appeared in British High Streets up and down the land. And if the cancer victim was now dead, the illness that had brought it to its knees was getting ready to wreak more havoc.

But what went wrong at Woolworths, and what could have been done to save it? Well, Woolworths had been struggling for some time, before its death, and had tried a number of ways to help improve its situation. But to implement radical changes, and to try and save a listing ship, you certainly need a crew able to meet the challenges. Gerald Corbett was appointed to oversee Woolworths demerger from Kingfisher, in 2001. Once the separation was complete, he stayed on at the company, until 2007, in the capacity of chairman. His tenure was an unspectacular one, and by the time he left the company its finances were in a perilous state. Corbett had tried his best to save the patient, and although he perhaps prolonged Woolworths life, the inevitable couldn't be avoided.

Only good people can get good results, which raises the question as to how Corbett actually found himself at the helm of the struggling retail giant. After all, his spell as Chief Executive of Railtrack, the privately owned operator of Britain's rail infrastructure, following the privatisation of British Rail, was one littered with disaster and poor management. During his short time at Railtrack, he oversaw three fatal rail accidents at Southall, Paddington and Hatfield. The total number of deaths amounted to forty-two, which resulted from shoddy management, poor controls and, worst of all, poor track maintenance. If people thought that the state-owned entity, that had been British Rail, had been bad, it was nowhere near as calamitous and tragic as Corbett's Railtrack. Corbett finally quit his employer with a handsome compensation package worth £1.3 million. Railtrack was eventually taken back into government control, in 2002, and rebranded Network Rail. Corbett's legacy was consigned to history, and his C.V. should have warned potential, future employers. It didn't, and shortly after leaving Railtrack he found himself in the top job at Woolworths. Barring a miracle, Woolworths was never going to work with him at the helm. By the time Corbett quit one of the High Street's most well-known occupiers, it was already entering its final death throes.

Of course, even the most spectacular managers can't make people buy things from their stores, but they can at least try. Whilst millions of us, myself included, still have nostalgia-fuelled flashbacks about the fallen giant, one has to admit that Woolworths really didn't move forward in time, as people were changing their shopping habits. The internet has really decimated a lot of retail-based businesses, but Woolworths problems were already apparent before the online-shopping craze kicked off. With Woolworths it was really a case of change or die. The giant didn't change its ways, so it died. It's as simple as that. Or, to put it another way, what worked well in the nineteen-seventies, in retail terms, doesn't work today. People want bright, open-spaced, well organised shops. They want quality goods at reasonable prices. As much as we talk about it, Woolworths was basically a big chain of shoddy-looking shops selling a lot of crap. It sold music, slippers and lottery tickets, together with Pick 'n' Mix sweets, light bulbs and batteries. At Christmastime, in its final years, it was still selling plastic Christmas trees, fairy lights and musical decorations. The chain really needed turning on its head and shaking violently. A more dynamic board of managers might have pulled off a great escape act, but Woolworths always seemed to be stuck in the past.

But crap clearly still has a place in our lives, as a large number of Woolworths vacant stores were taken over by Poundland – purveyors of absolute rubbish at amazing prices. If Poundland lives for a hundred years it will be a great feat, and it means it will outlive Woolworths by at least ten months. It will mean that people still want cheap and cheerful tat, that they can't buy cheaper elsewhere. Investors and potential buyers were still trying to save the wounded beast up to its final days, but to no avail. And sadly, unlike a cricketer who's out for ninety-nine, but who can always come back in the next match and make a century, this is one player who's gone for good. Frank Woolworth must have turned in his grave, the day his baby died. He must have looked down at that big pile of debt, and wondered where it had all gone wrong. It was good while it lasted, but nothing good lasts forever.

And with one giant dead and buried, other big names have either followed Woolworths into oblivion, or, in the case of Marks & Spencer, they're having to adapt to survive, with their glory years long behind them. Woolworths was big, but Marks & Spencer was bigger. Woolworths has gone, and, albeit through massive scaling back, reinventing itself and changing the way it operates, Marks & Spencer is still hanging on, even if it is a shadow of its former self. It's been poorly for some time, it's lost a lot of weight, but it refuses to go.

Founded in 1884, in Leeds, by two friends, the company was run as a penny-bazaar, with a more than original advertising slogan. DON'T ASK THE PRICE, EVERYTHING'S A PENNY was the crowd-puller, as the two partners opened up market stalls throughout the north-west of England. Expansion was rapid, and near the end of the 1920's the famous St. Michael brand was introduced. Further domestic expansion followed, before, in the mid-1970's, the company's first foray in Europe saw it open stores on the continent.

The company, by now growing at an impressive rate, was in the safe hands of Israel Sieff, the son-in-law of Simon Marks, who was the son of one of the company's original founders, Michael Marks. And this was really the most important time for the company, and probably the beginning of its golden period, in which it really dominated Britain's High Streets. Sieff, in turn, would be replaced by Edward and Marcus Sieff, before Derek Rayner took over the reigns of the company in 1984.

By the mid-1970's the company was already selling the frozen food that, although at the time seemed perhaps too exotic for British tastes, would provide the springboard for its enhanced range of food products. Frozen lamb curry, lasagne, pizza and Chinese food, to be commonly known as convenience food, could be bought at many of the company's stores, with Marks & Spencer becoming the first British retailer in 1979 to sell Chicken Kiev in its stores. It may seem quite laughable now, when we think of the innovations that Marks & Spencer was behind, but back in the seventies this was really as good as it got. And if the food was bringing in the customers through the doors, there was also the company's vast range of clothing.

The company was now a global monster, with more than forty stores in Canada, and branches in France and Belgium. And if the seventies were kind to the company, the following decade would bring even more success. New stores were being opened, more jobs being created and certainly more money being made. Towards the end of the eighties the company bought the American clothing company, Brooks Brothers. And on the beast rolled, under Richard Greenbury's command, trundling into the nineties like an unstoppable juggernaut, when, in 1998, it announced record pre-tax profits of £1,155 billion on a turnover of £8,243 billion. Figures that made other retailers sit up and take notice. A performance of eye-watering dimensions, proving that Marks & Spencer wasn't only the King of the High Street, but that it was, in all honesty, THE High Street. And then it all went terribly wrong.

On my most recent visit to a Marks & Spencer store, in the winter of 2020, to buy a pair of moccasins, the first thing that struck me was that I appeared to have travelled back in time. My wife looked at the clothes in the ladies clothing department, and came to the conclusion that what should have been in, was nowhere to be seen in the shop. The menswear department was equally depressing, only matched by the lack of lighting throughout the store. If it was a dull and gloomy day outside, then it wasn't much brighter inside amongst the terrible suits and shirts that I passed, on the way to finding my moccasins.

Fashion has almost killed off Marks & Spencer – or, more accurately, the failure to keep up with what's in, and to jettison what's not. On the food front, there can be no complaints. But, in all honesty, it's just too expensive. I'd rather buy a sherry trifle from Tesco, although more people are buying food from Marks & Spencer, explaining why their food-only stores seem to be saving its skin. But what about the most important thing, for any retailer – what about it's figures? Well, if 1998 was its golden year, things have been getting slowly worse ever since. Apart from a short-lived rebound in 2008, the company's recent performance is depressing, to say the least. In 2018 its after-tax profit was £29 million, the following year it was slightly better at £37 million, and, in a Covid-ravaged year, the profits slumped to £27 million. Of course, the Covid-19 outbreak has done nothing to help the world's overall economy, but the men and women running Marks & Spencer today know that the company was already struggling, years before.

The rot had already set in, in 2004, when the company was limping along like a lame dog. It was at this time that it managed to stave off a bid from Philip Green's Arcadia group. Green saw himself as a saviour, but mercifully he wasn't able to get his hands on the company. Since then, and this is another story entirely, Green's own empire has come crashing down around him. He is the man who single-handedly drove British Home Stores into the ground, and he is the man who could do nothing to save his Top Shop empire. For Marks & Spencer, it was a blessing that they fought off the tacky and vulgar Green. But when the dust settled, they knew changes had to be made.

After regular changes of senior management in the company, over the last two decades, no real inroads have been made into bringing back the glory years. Perhaps too arrogant to see that its customers would never think of shopping elsewhere, and certainly too blind to see the changing landscape, Marks & Spencer has acted too late to drag itself into the new millennium. Its online store is okay, but it's not fantastic. It seems to be throwing itself into the extremely cut-throat food-only market, where the competition is fierce. And when once the company was opening stores at a breath-taking rate, today, in an attempt to make it a leaner and slicker machine, the company is in the throes of a massive restructuring plan, closing stores along the way.

In my home-town of Deal, in Kent, where the High Street is split into two halves, the old Woolworths store is now occupied by Poundland. In the other half, where Marks & Spencer once stood proud, there is just a vacant store, empty of life and frozen curries. Needless to say, Deal High Street is a shadow of its former self, occupied by a few coffee shops and some other almost-dead retailers. The Saurdays of yesterday are long gone, just like Woolworths, Debenhams, Top Shop and many other retailers.

There'll be no comebacks on the High Street, and that is certain. Some big names are gone, and others are struggling. Be it because of the Internet, or our changing habits, it's difficult to say, but it's tragic to think that perhaps in no more than five to ten years from now, Britain's High Streets will be pedestrianised graveyards.

Ask a French person to give their thoughts on Britain, and they will usually reply that the food is crap, it always rains, we have no sense of style, Benny Hill was great and pubs are even greater. It's sad to see that the only good things we are renowned for is a comedian, whose shows in the eighties involved sexy young ladies popping up every thirty seconds, and ale houses. Benny Hill, sadly, is long gone, and if we can still watch his shows on nostalgia-fuelled television satellite channels, his brand of comedy is outdated. What made us laugh forty years ago might raise laughs from devotees of the Southampton-born showman, but a younger generation would probably find it embarrassingly unfunny. And what about the British pub? What about that iconic entity that is as British as fish and chips or roast beef and Yorkshire puddings?

In my home-town there were a lot of pubs, when I was a kid. In fact, in the vicinity of my childhood home, there was a ridiculously large number of them within walking distance. Head over the fields, towards Sholden, and you'd arrive at The Sportsman, a thatched-roof, village pub with a gentle and cosy interior and a delightful beer garden. The floor was nicely carpeted, there were brass objects hanging up and there were no fruit machines or televisions showing live football matches. It's the sort of pub that tourists would want to take photos of, to show the folks at home just what a British pub looks like. The last time I drank there was over twenty-five years ago, when it had been taken over by a Geordie man and wife team, who had left the north-east of England to try their hand at running a genteel establishment, in the Garden of England. The pub they had run in the other end of the country was nothing like The Sportsman. There were no armies of lager drinkers standing ten deep, at the bar, knocking back pints of Stella Artois and talking football. No, this was a pub where old folk nursed their pints of bitter, and others drank white wine whilst eating their Sunday lunch.

Now let's leave The Sportsman, walk down the main road, back towards Deal, and call in at The Admiral Keppel. I'm a fast walker, so in five minutes I've covered the distance that separates the two watering holes. We're now in Upper Deal, and a pub that is a world away from the twee world of The Sportsman. This is what you would call a "real" pub, with its music, fruit machines, pool table and a charity jar at the end of the bar, in which drinkers would empty their copper coins. Not a thatched roof here, and the pub was just set back from a busy main road. If you drank too much on a Friday night, and fell off the pavement, the chances are that you could have been run over by a car or bus. The Keppel, as it was commonly referred to, was a man's pub, whereas The Sportsman was a family pub. It attracted a different class of customer, On a busy Friday night it would be packed with people wanting to drink and play pool, or pour money into a fruit machine. On a busy Friday night at The Sportsman, the restaurant, which shared the same space as the bar, would be full of middle-aged and old couples eating their paté and toast starters, whilst the chef prepared their scampi and chips main course. They would be drinking red wine and listening to the quiet background music.

Anyway, where is all of this heading? Well, if you left The

Keppel, and walked back towards my childhood home, you would pass The Magnet, and then, walking on for another short distance, you would pass The Bowling Green. Carry on for a few hundred yards and I would be home, but continue for another couple of hundred yards, in a straight line, and I'd find myself at another pub. So that's at least five pubs in a couple of square miles. Ridiculous, indeed, for a town of Deal's size. And I haven't even mentioned the town centre or seafront, which was jam-packed with all sorts of pubs.

Yet in the seventies and eighties, and indeed earlier, these pubs were raking money in. And don't forget that this was in a time when opening hours were prehistoric. The idea that was all-day opening didn't see the light until 1988, prior to which pubs were required to close in the afternoon, before reopening for the evening. I remember as a small child sometimes going to The Sportsman, with my parents and brother on a Sunday lunchtime. Mum and dad would be in the bar, drinking their Cinzano and lemonade and pint of bitter. We would be served our soft drinks through a serving hatch, which looked out onto the beer garden. Children, then, were not allowed in the bar, so we would kick around a football until the time came for us to go home. The pub would then close, and reopen in the evening for a few hours. This was in the late seventies, when my Dad was working hard in a local factory. Our visits to the pub were few and far between, because with two boys to raise, drinking beer wasn't really possible financially. Okay, a pint of bitter in 1976, when Britain was basking in a heatwave, cost on average thirty-two pence. Whoooaaa, don't get too excited, because the average weekly wage for a man was £70. I know that my Dad (may he rest in peace) wasn't taking home that every week. In his job at the factory, his take-home pay was significantly lower, which meant that by the time the rent had been paid, the bills taken care of, the weekly shopping had been bought and he had got his rolling tobacco, there wasn't much money left. And when the Winter of Discontent kicked in, and his working hours were reduced, money was even tighter. A trip to the pub for him, and many others, was a luxury.

But the pubs throughout the land kept on going, because when the chips are down, life is hard, and money is tight, the British have always used their local watering hole as a place of comfort, where they can escape from the harsh realities of life. It sounds perverted that a man who is broke needs to go to a pub, to get hammered on beer or spirits, to forget his problems, in the process putting himself into even more debt. I, myself, have endured some very difficult moments, financially. But after a trip to the pub, for a few pints and cigarettes, everything always seemed to be not so bad. In the nineties, when I had a well-paid job, I used to work opposite a pub. I'd be in there every lunchtime, and sometimes in the evening, after work, knocking back pints of lager. I shudder to think I have blown on lager and whisky, in pubs, in my lifetime, in pursuit of some feel-good moments. I wouldn't like to imagine how much money I've poured into fruit machines during the course of my life. I reckon it runs into thousands of pounds, but gambling, like boozing, is just another way to forget one's problems. Yet it's people like me who kept the pubs going. In Deal, on a Friday night, the town's pubs would be at the point of bursting. If you could get through the doors, and make it through the cloud of cigarette smoke, to the bar, you were doing well. If your voice could be heard above the din, as you asked for two pints of lager, you were doing either better.

Benny Hill was at his peak in the eighties. His smut-laced humour was pulling in the viewers. At the end of the eighties there were approximately 64,000 pubs in Britain. A decade later, after the end of the boom and bust period of Thatcher's government, that number had dropped to approximately 61,000, whilst Benny Hill's success ran out of steam in 1989. In 2010, thirty years after Thatcher's revolution began, there were 55,000 pubs in Britain. In 2019 the number of pubs has dwindled away to 47,000, with the number in rapid decline since the Covid-19 pandemic. But we can't blame everything on Covid-19 and its repercussions, can we?

Well, all good things must come to an end. Covid-19 has certainly been a massive kick in the balls for pubs and the hospitality industry in Britain, and almost everywhere else in the world, and it's certain that, like the High Street, there's not going to be a resurgence. The chances are that once a pub is boarded up and left to rot, that's how it stays. The sad truth is that people fell out of love with pubs years ago. That British tradition has lost its sparkle and allure, and now people want different things. On Twitter many of my followers post tweets of them extolling the virtues of the latest real ale or micro-brewery made beer. But they don't post their tweets from the inside of pubs, they post photos of the latest offering, whether it be in a can or a bottle, which they drink from the comfort of their own homes. That's the big revolution that will bring the axe crashing down on many other pubs in the near future. And as in all walks of life, for every loser there's got to be a winner. Just take a look at the beer aisle of your local supermarket, and you'll be dazzled by the sheer selection on offer. Ten years ago it was lager and bitter, whereas today it's all about real ales and international beers. The prices are attractive, and with their financial clout, the supermarkets can offer incredible price deals. During the Covid-19 lockdowns, when pubs were forced to stay shut, the supermarkets knew that they had a captive audience. Sadly for the pubs, when they were allowed to reopen, their customer base had changed its drinking habits. Most people, but not all, realised that drinking at home has its advantages – it's certainly cheaper and the atmosphere is probably calmer. If we were happy, when we were eighteen, to stand in a crowded pub, shouting at the top of our voices, whilst watching people throw up on the carpet, in our fifties we desire peace and quiet. I certainly don't want to stand in a pub with a load of spotty teenagers, who seem to drink as if lager is about to go out of fashion.

And from the comfort of our own home, whilst drinking our beer or wine, there's something else that we're free to do, that we can no longer do in pubs. The pub trade was mortally wounded on the 1st July 2007, when a law came into effect making it illegal to smoke in the interior of pubs, restaurants, cafés, nightclubs and most workplaces. I stopped smoking twenty years ago, so this new law was welcomed by people like me. Before, however, I would get through a packet of cigarettes in an evening, in a pub, whilst knocking back copious amounts of lager. Drinking and smoking went hand in hand. I would order a pint and light my first cigarette. Thinking about it, smoking is probably the most antisocial habit practised by man. To ban smoking in pubs was probably a right thing to do, on health grounds, but its effect on the pub industry has been devastating. To ask someone to pay over five pounds for a pint of whatever is already demanding a lot, to then ask them to stand outside on the pavement, in the rain, to smoke is really taking the biscuit. The smoking ban really decimated the hospitality industry, with pubs taking a huge battering. Covid-19 has just more or less hammered the final nails into the coffin.

The last time I went into a pub, in England, it was rather a depressing experience. There were two old men sat at the bar, nursing their pints. Then there was my wife and me – and nobody else. The barmaid was friendly enough, which was a good thing, as I handed over fifteen pounds for a pint of Guinness and a large glass of white wine. It was a pub that I was familiar with, as I used to frequent it when I was younger. On a Saturday lunchtime, back then, it would have been bursting at the seams. Twenty years later it was dying on its feet. I ordered another two drinks, and handed over another fifteen pounds. I had now spent thirty pounds for four drinks. In the 1970's you could have watered a football team with that sort of money, but those days are long gone.

Logically, and sadly, there will be no comeback for the pub industry. What was good forty years ago is today considered no longer essential. Britain is in a terrible mess, with people struggling to feed their families. Food banks are sprouting up all over the land, as working people find it necessary to rely on handouts to keep going. People are employed with zero-hour contracts. You can be in work in the morning, and unemployed in the afternoon. There is no job security, and indeed good jobs are hard to find. The cost of living in Britain, like in many other countries, is constantly rising, whilst wages aren't increasing. Once the bills are paid, food has been bought, the mortgage or rent has been paid, and petrol put in the car, there's not much money left. Pubs have become a victim of the changing times, and drinking in them is now a luxury that most of us cannot afford.

I hope you enjoyed reading this book. You can follow the author, on Twitter, @YesterdaysBrit1

By the same author:

'Whatever Will Be, Will Be'

'Whatever Will Be, Will Be'

The sequel to *'Trudging Through Yesterday's Britain'*

Introduction.

Five...four...three...two...one...Happy New Year! And as the first second of the year 2000 came and went in the blink of an eye, the three previous decades that I had somehow safely negotiated – often drunk, poor and hopelessly lost – now seemed further away than they actually were. The seventies, eighties and nineties weren't only the last thirty years, but now they were also part of the previous millennium – that thousand-year stretch of time that was mentally reset to zero, when the first moments of the new thousand-year stretch were welcomed with champagne, balloons, fireworks, jolly music and the world and its mother kissing the world and its mother on the mouth, or the cheeks, and singing, dancing, drinking more champagne, guzzling beer, swigging whisky, slurping red wine and eating fancy-cut sandwiches, that pretty girls in sexy outfits were doling out. And I drank anything and everything that evening, and I stuffed those sandwiches down my throat, and I kissed strangers and I sang out loud. And I was happy – VERY happy!

But nothing good lasts forever, and the next day – when computer engineers had feared a massive technological meltdown would bring the world shuddering to a halt – the only thing that was really bothering me was the massive hangover that I had woken up with, and that would accompany me throughout that first day of the new millennium. That bastard pounding sensation was something that I was familiar with, but this one was the biggest I had known for some time. At noon I ate bacon sandwiches, drank beer and took two paracetamol tablets, and it was only later on in the day did the thumping fizzle out. And if I had planned to go for a long walk to clear my head, I instead returned to the comfort of my bed, where I stayed until the second day of the new year came and woke me.

For those of you who are familiar with the first part of my memoirs, *Trudging Through Yesterday's Britain,* you will know that me making it through the previous thirty years had hardly been a walk in the park, or a joy-ride. I hadn't sailed through those years graciously, and when I thought that I was doing okay, there was always someone, somewhere, to cause me problems along the way. I had tried my best to do something with my life, but every time I moved three steps forward I would usually go four steps back. But trudging along, with my head up and me looking forward, was all that I could do, if I was to make something of my life. And because I was a natural-born trudger, there would be no other way for me to go about things. Believe me, I would have liked to have blazed a trail or set the world on fire, but I wasn't born with trail-blazing instincts. Instead I was put on this earth to just edge along, seeing what I could achieve with the character I had been born with, and the guile that I developed along the way.

The summer of 1976 is the first big thing that comes to my mind when I think about my childhood. The years before are a bit of a blur now, but I do have some vague memories of what happened around me during the years preceding that golden summer. At the end of the seventies I would leave primary school and move on to a new school – an awful place in which I was compelled to spend the five most miserable years of my life. Deal Secondary School and its bastard teachers is something I still have nightmares about, with me dreaming in monochrome that I must go back there, to endure another five-year spell, because I hadn't done great things the first time I had been there. The walk from home to school was okay in the summertime, but whenever it was raining it just piled on the misery. And in my nocturnal flashbacks it only ever rains.

Fortunately, my schooling is behind me, and if those years had been difficult, *Trudging Through Yesterday's Britain* tells the story of my continual struggle to find a decent job, in the sea of opportunity that was the eighties. There were highs and there were lows, in a time when Britain seemed to offer so much hope and promise. Then the eighties turned into the nineties, and things started to change in Yesterday's Britain. It was a new decade, and new ways and new days were on the horizon. But still I moved along, although never surely and often clumsily, until I found THE job that had eluded me for so long. And when I finally settled into my new employment, I did so with the belief that from that moment on, in 1993, everything was finally going right for me. And to start with it did, and even if I encountered a few problems in the early days of my new career, it felt like that everything had finally slotted into place and that I had finally achieved what I had set out to do many years before.

Trudging Through Yesterday's Britain ends at pretty much the same time as 1999 was coming to an end, and if I was looking forward to the coming new year, I did so knowing that the job that I had pinned so many hopes on was also coming to an end. Yes – the carpet had been pulled out from under my feet, and I was soon to be joining the ranks of the unemployed. So it was really a case of out with the old, in all aspects of my life, as the world was excitedly preparing for the arrival of the year 2000, and all that would come with it. The parties up and down the land, and the world over, on the very last day of the soon-to-be old millennium would be extra special, with so much emphasis being placed on what the next thousand years would bring to the world, and how the last thousand years had moulded and shaped the lives of every man, woman and child on the planet.

So what became of me in those early few days of January 2000, and what were my plans and intentions for the future? Would it be more of the same, or would I take a giant leap into the unknown? Would I continue to trudge through life in my safe and steady way, or would I throw caution to the wind, and adopt a couldn't-care-a-less attitude? And if a radical change was coming, would it really be so bad if I was to fail in my new life? After all, we only live once, and when life is over, it's over.

I'm glad that I was born at a time when the following years would be some of the best that Britain has ever known. Yesterday's Britain really was a better Britain, and a different Britain to the one we know today. I was lucky to have been around in the eighties, when I set out on the road to employment. I certainly wouldn't want to be sixteen today, in a country that seems to have lost its way in the world. I feel sorry for today's young generation, because those people are going to have a hard time in making something of their lives.

This is the second part of my memoirs, in which my story continues from where *Trudging Through Yesterday's Britain* ends. We cannot deny that we're all masters of our own destiny, although I also believe that our lives are mapped out for us from the very day when we are born. But whether our futures aren't of our own making, or it is us who choose which path to take, it's better to have tried, and failed, than never to have tried at all. And if we never quite catch that golden star, that hangs over all of our heads, it doesn't really matter, because that's the way life goes. And when we're dead, we're dead, and whatever will be, will be.

'*Whatever Will Be, Will Be*' is now available from Amazon, in Kindle & paperback version.